DRAW 50

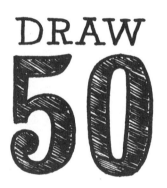

ATHLETES

The Step-by-Step Way to Draw
Wrestlers and Figure Skaters, Baseball
and Football Players, and Many More . . .

BOOKS IN THIS SERIES

DRAW 50 | ATHLETES

The Step-by-Step Way to Draw Wrestlers and Figure Skaters, Baseball and Football Players, and Many More . . .

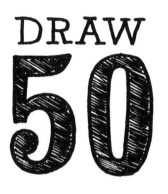

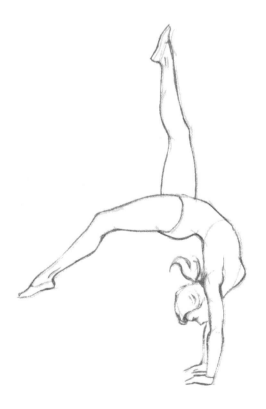

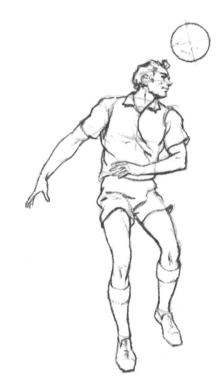

LEE J. AMES

Watson-Guptill Publications, New York

All rights reserved.
Published in the United States by Watson-Guptill Publications,
an imprint of the Crown Publishing Group, a division of Random
House, Inc., New York, in 2012.
www.crownpublishing.com

WATSON-GUPTILL and the WG and Horse designs are
registered trademarks of Random House, Inc.

Originally published in hardcover in the United States by
Doubleday, a division of Random House, Inc., New York, in 1985.

Library of Congress Cataloging-in-Publication Data

Ames, Lee J.
    Draw 50 athletes.
    [62]p. :chiefly ill.; 32 cm.
    Summary: Step-by-step instructions on how to draw a variety
of athletes from a number of action perspectives.
    1. Action in art—Juvenile literature. 2. Athletes in art—Juvenile
literature. 3. Wrestlers in art—Juvenile literature. 4. Drawing—
Techniques—Juvenile literature. [1. Athletes in art. 2. Drawing—
Technique] I. Title. II. Title: Draw fifty athletes.
    NC785.A46   1985   743'.4   83.45569

ISBN 978-0-8230-8572-9
eISBN 978-0-307-98562-0

Printed in the United States of America

10 9 8 7 6 5 4 3 2 1

To Jonathan and Cindy,
my favorite athletes,
with much love . . .

. . . and thanks to Warren Budd for all his help.

To the Reader

This book of 50 athletes will show you a method of drawing the human figure, of searching out the basic simple forms and lightly building one on the other. When these forms add up to a complete figure, drawn very lightly up to this point, the drawing is finished with firm, dark lines.

You need not start with the first illustration. Choose whichever you wish. When you have decided, follow the step-by-step method shown. *Very lightly* and *carefully*, sketch out step number one. However, this step, which is the easiest, should be done *most carefully*. Step number two is added right to step number one, also lightly and also very carefully. Step number 3 is sketched right on top of numbers one and two. Continue this way to the last step.

It may seem strange to ask you to be extra careful when you are drawing what seem to be the easiest first steps, but this is most important, for a careless mistake at the beginning may spoil the whole picture at the end. As you sketch out each step, watch the spaces between the lines, as well as the lines, and see that they are the same. After each step, you may want to lighten your work by pressing it with a kneaded eraser (available at art supply stores).

When you have finished, you may want to redo the final step in India ink with a fine brush or pen. When the ink is dry, use the kneaded eraser to clean off the pencil lines. The eraser will not affect the India ink.

Here are some suggestions: In the first few steps, even

when all seems quite correct, you might do well to hold your work up to a mirror. Sometimes the mirror shows that you've twisted the drawing off to one side without being aware of it. At first you may find it difficult to draw the egg shapes, or ball shapes, or sausage shapes, or just to make the pencil go where you wish. Don't be discouraged. The more you practice, the more you will develop control. The only equipment you'll need will be a medium or soft pencil, paper, the kneaded eraser and, if you wish, a pen or brush and India ink.

The first steps in this book are shown darker than necessary so that they can be clearly seen. (Keep your work very light)

Remember there are many other ways and methods to make drawings. This book shows just one method. Why don't you seek out other ways from teachers, from libraries and, most importantly . . . from inside yourself?

Lee J. Ames

To the Parent or Teacher

"Leslie can draw a soccer player better than anybody else!" Such peer acclaim and encouragement generate incentive. Contemporary methods of art instruction (freedom of expression, experimentation, self-evaluation of competence and growth) provide a vigorous, fresh-air approach for which we must all be grateful.

New ideas need not, however, totally exclude the old. One such is the "follow me, step-by-step" approach. In my young learning days this method was so common, and frequently so exclusive, that the student became nothing more than a pantographic extension of the teacher. In those days it was excessively overworked.

This does not mean that the young hand is never to be guided. Rather, specific guiding is fundamental. Step-by-step guiding that produces satisfactory results is valuable even when the means of accomplishment are not fully understood by the student.

The novice with a musical instrument is frequently taught to play simple melodies as quickly as possible, well before he learns the most elemental scratchings at the surface of music theory. The resultant self-satisfaction, pride in accomplishment, can be a significant means of providing motivation. And all from mimicking an instructor's "Do-as-I-do. . . ."

Mimicry is prerequisite for developing creativity. We learn the use of our tools by mimicry. Then we can use those tools for creativity. To this end I would offer the budding artist the opportunity to memorize or mimic (rotelike, if you wish) the making of "pictures." "Pictures" he has been eager to be able to draw.

The use of this book should be available to anyone who *wants* to try another way of flapping his wings. Perhaps he will then get off the ground when his friend says, "Leslie can draw a soccer player better than anyone else!"

Lee J. Ames

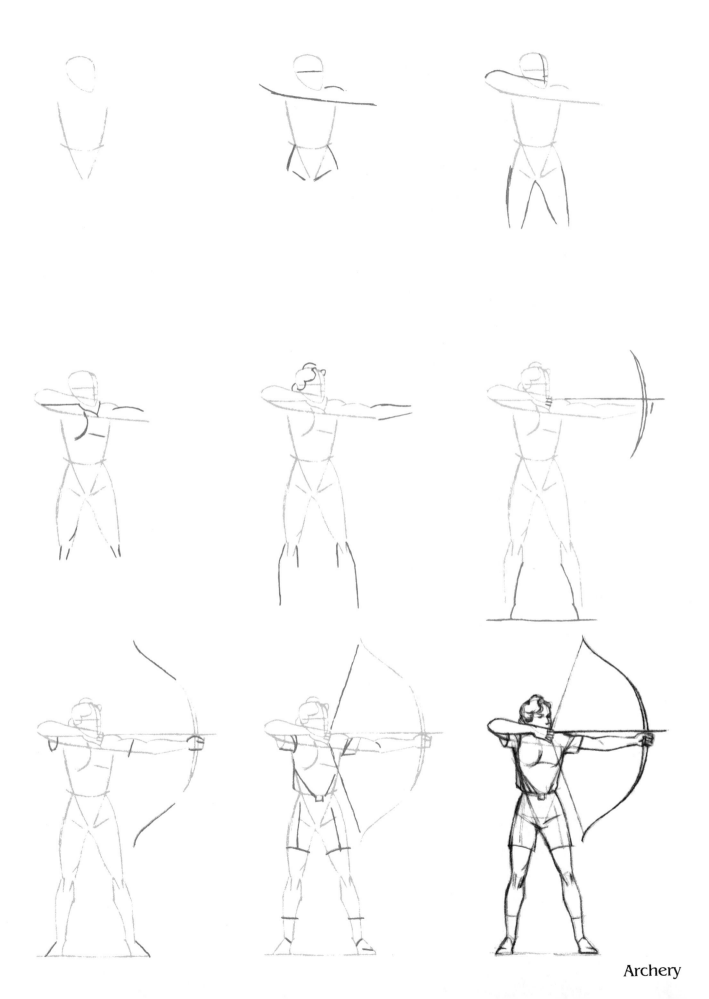

Archery

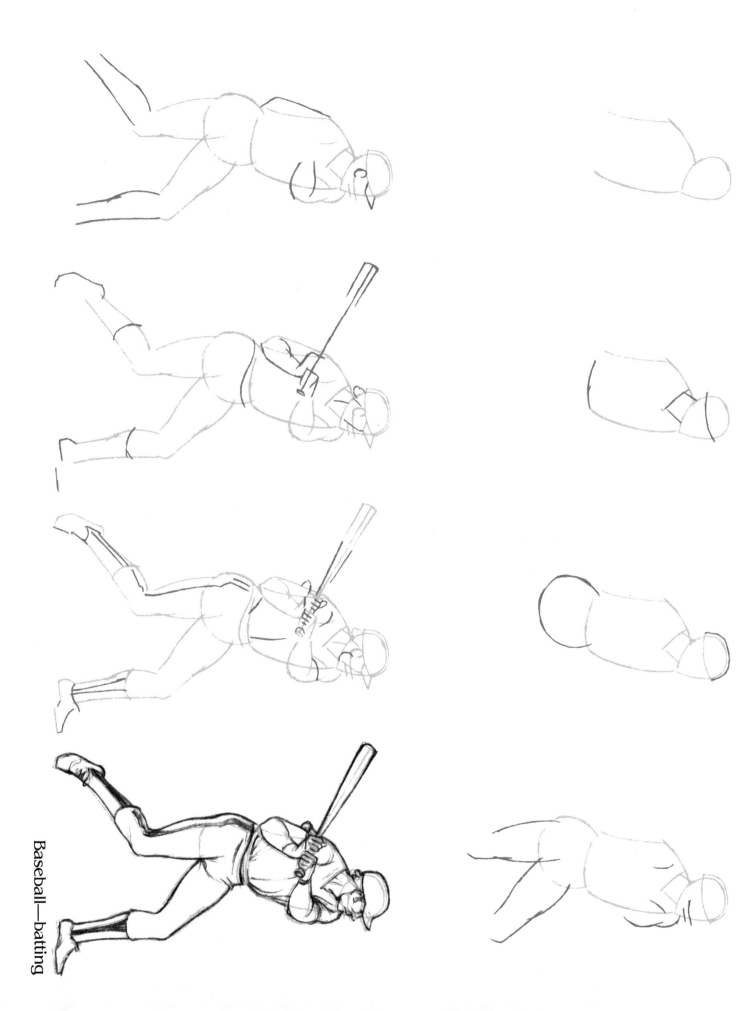

Baseball—batting

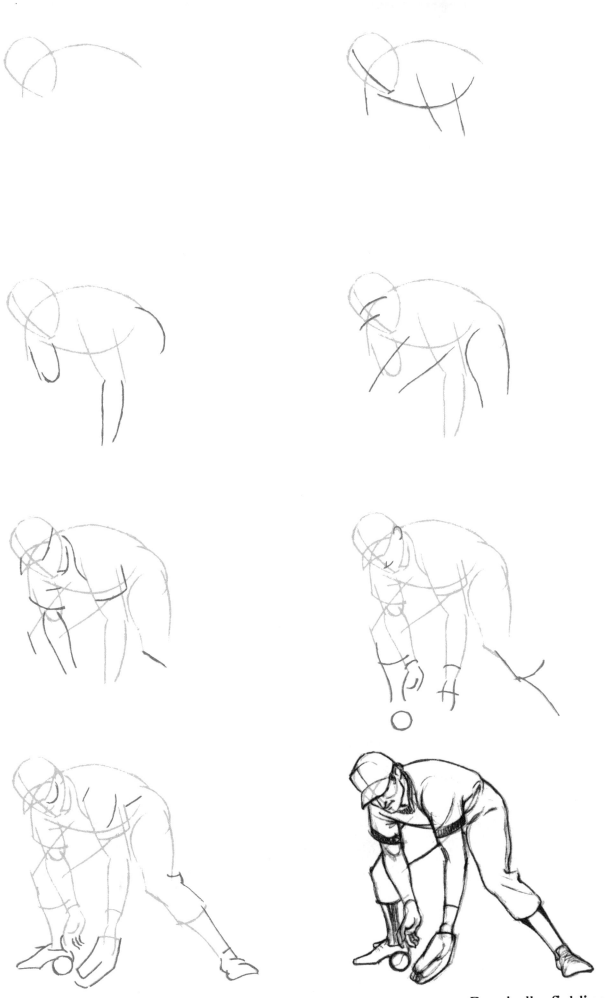

Baseball—fielding

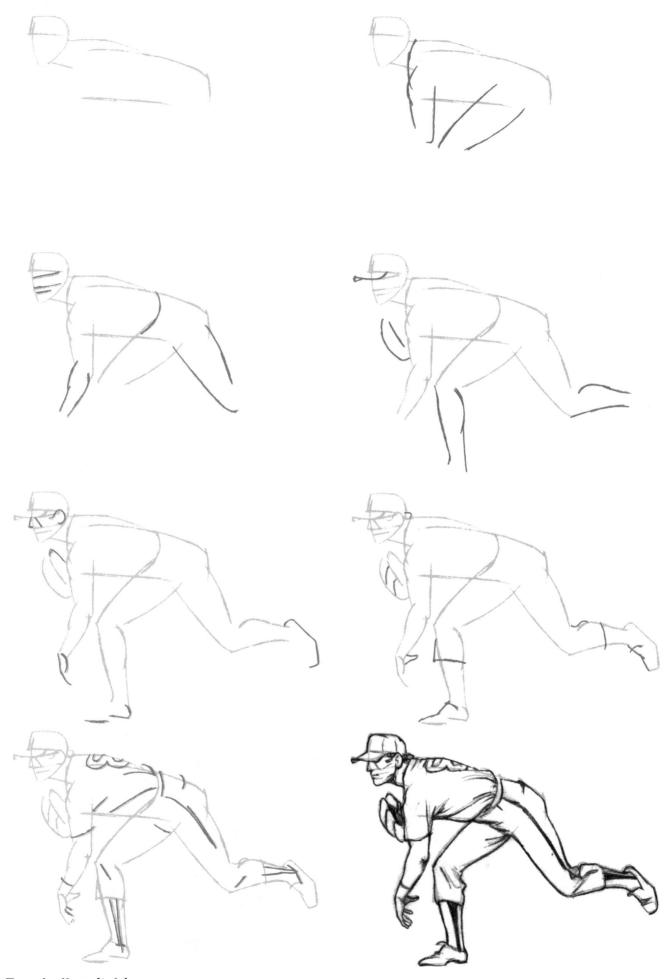

Baseball—pitching

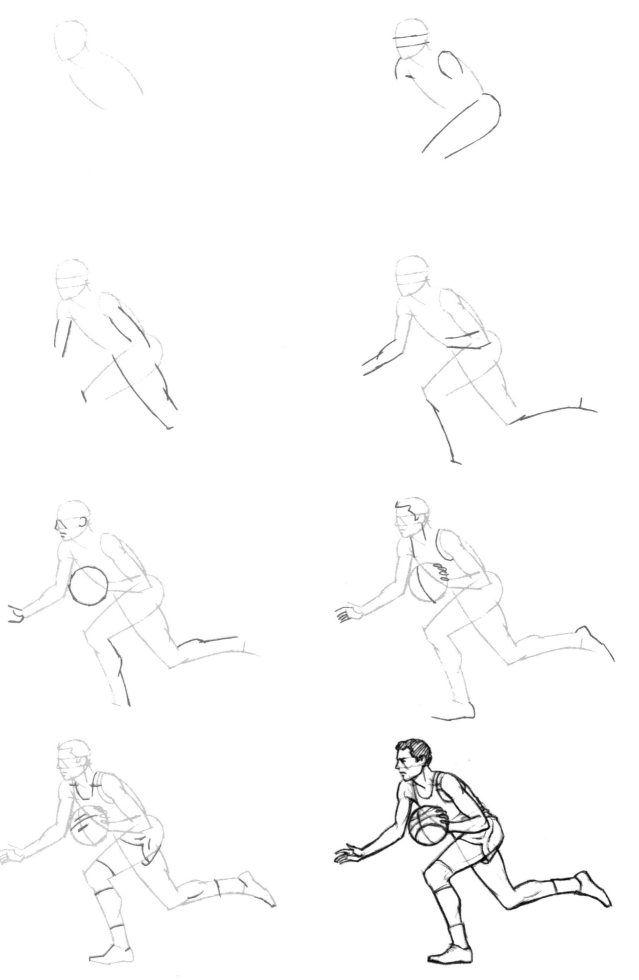

Basketball—dribbling

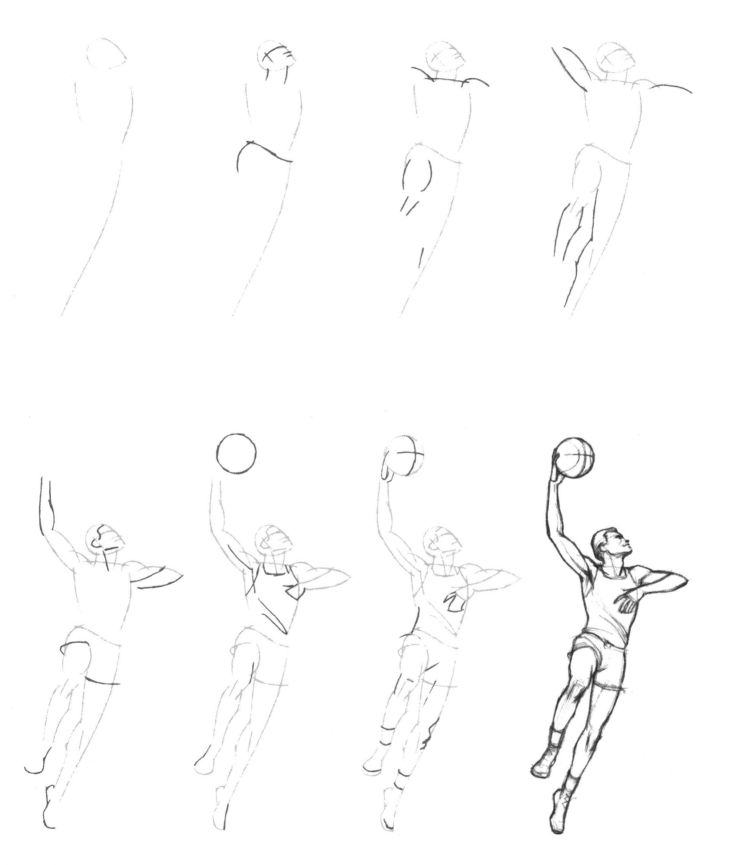

Basketball—hook shot

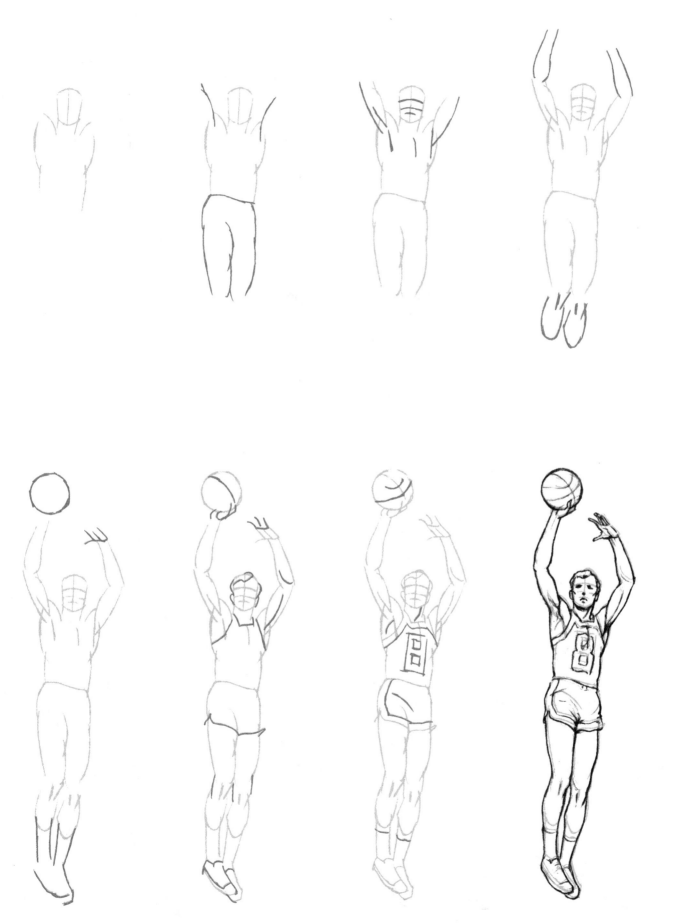

Basketball—jump shot

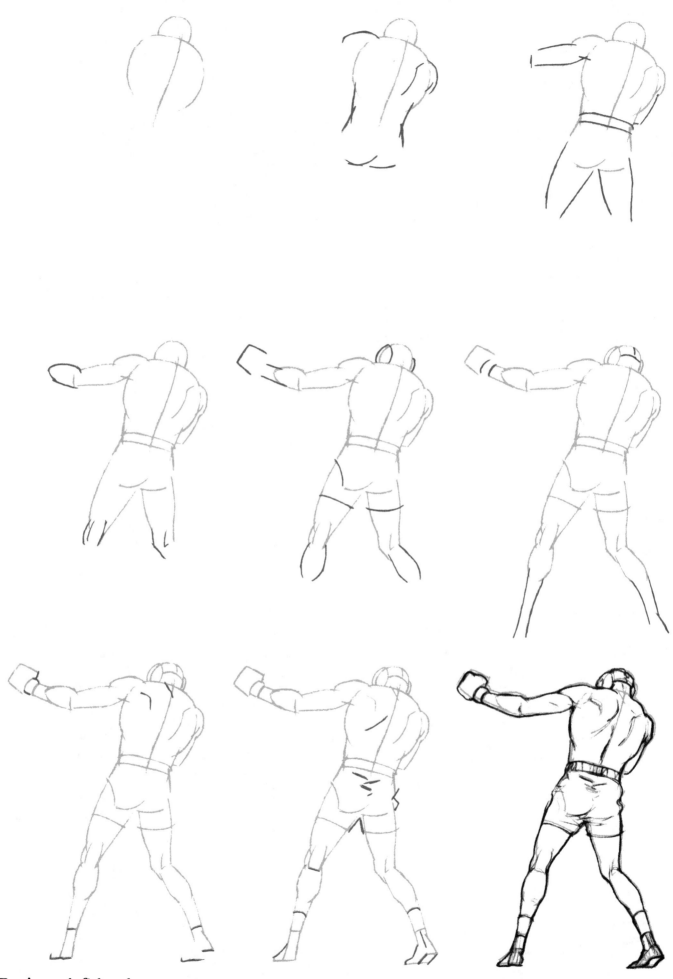

Boxing—left hook

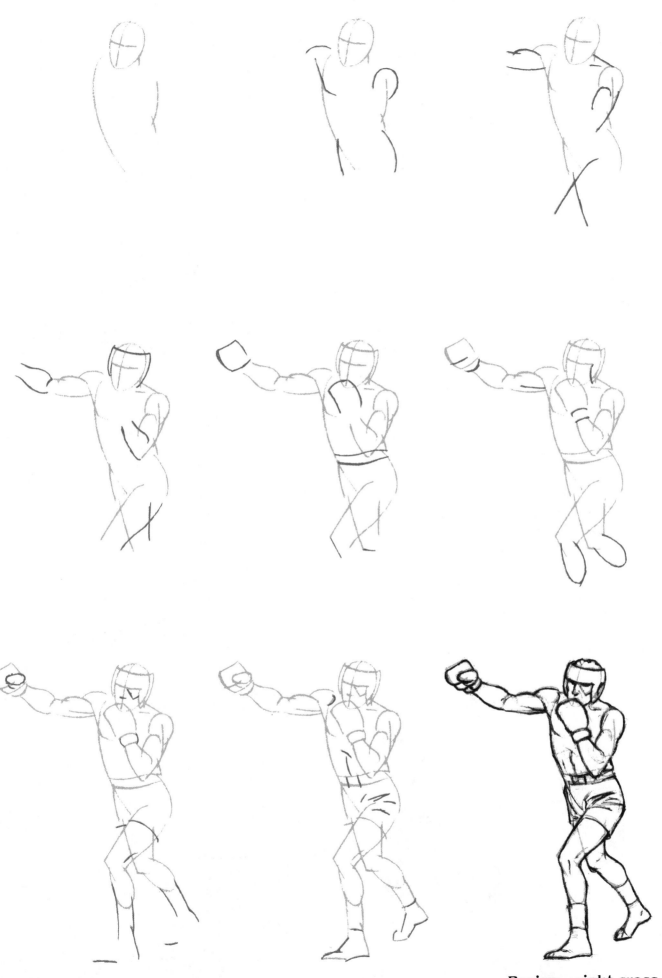

Boxing—right cross

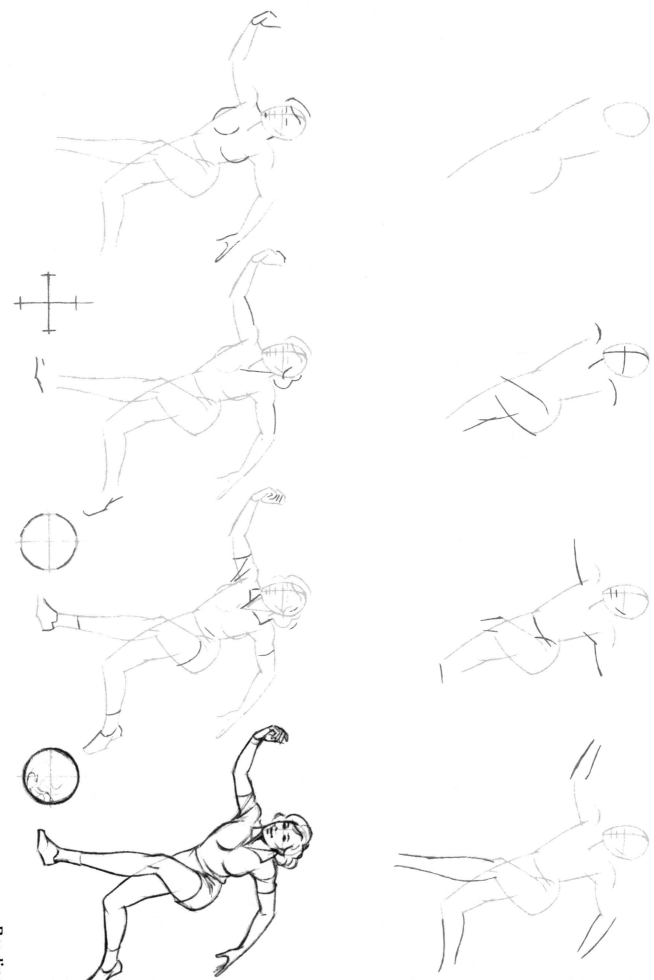

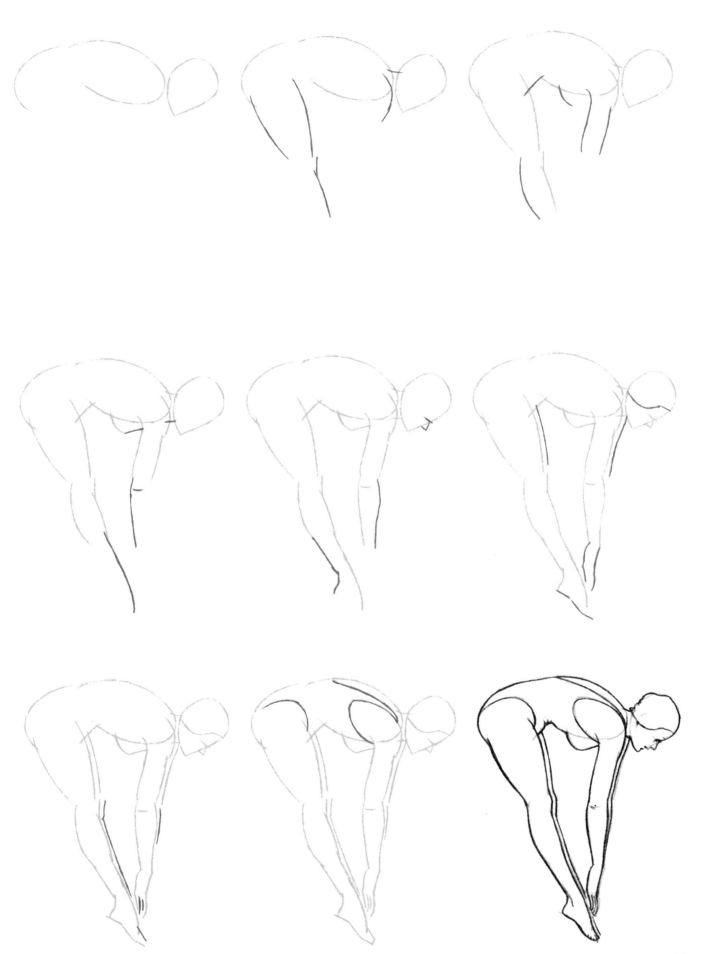

Diving—jacknife

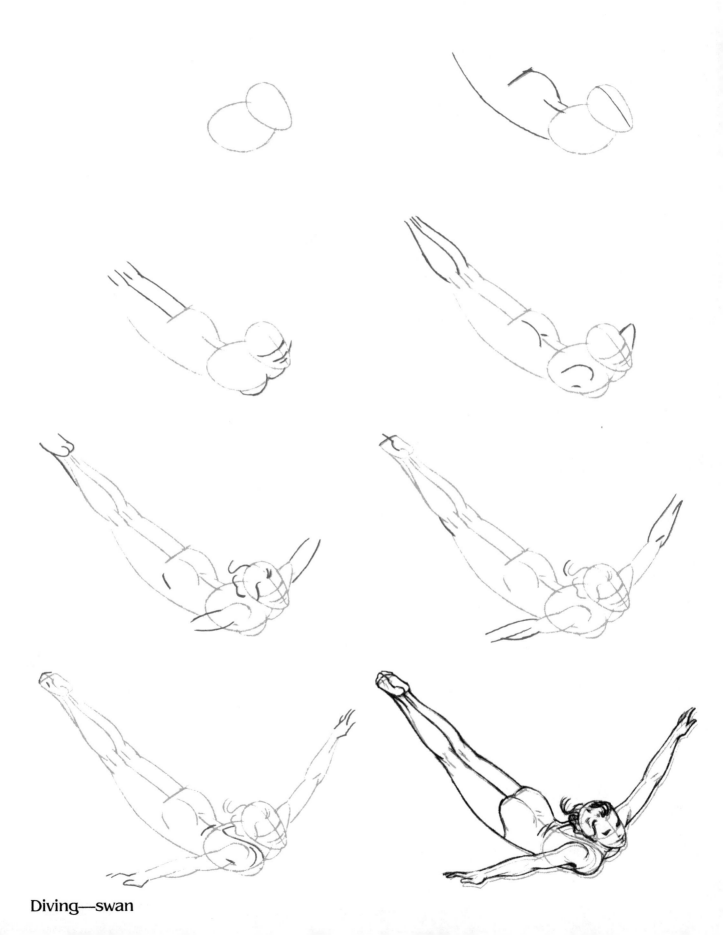

Diving—swan

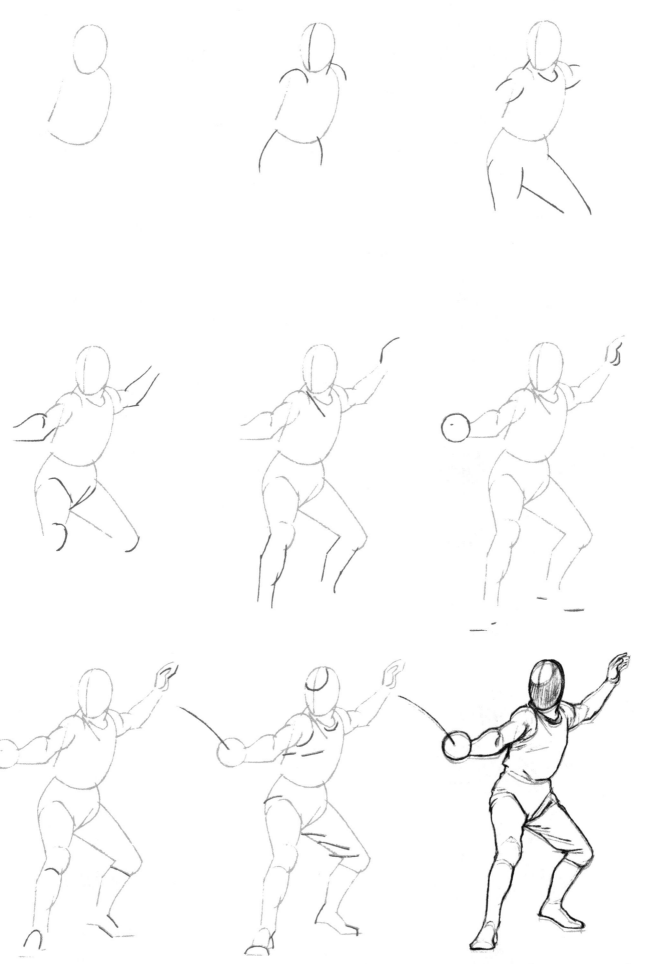

Fencing—en garde

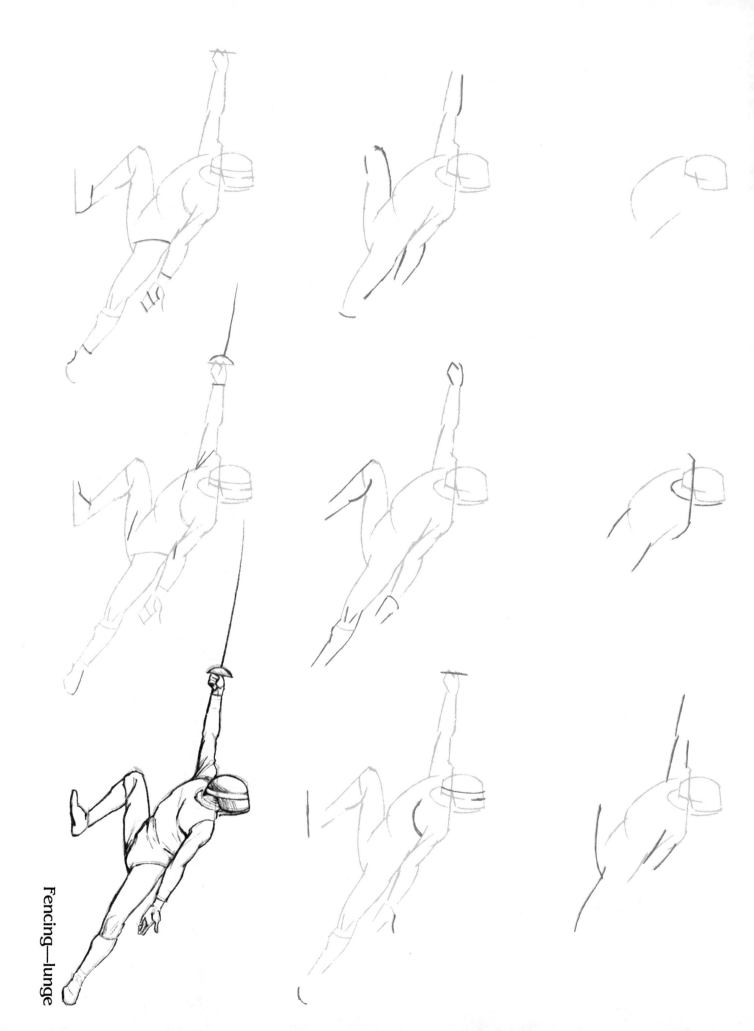

Fencing—lunge

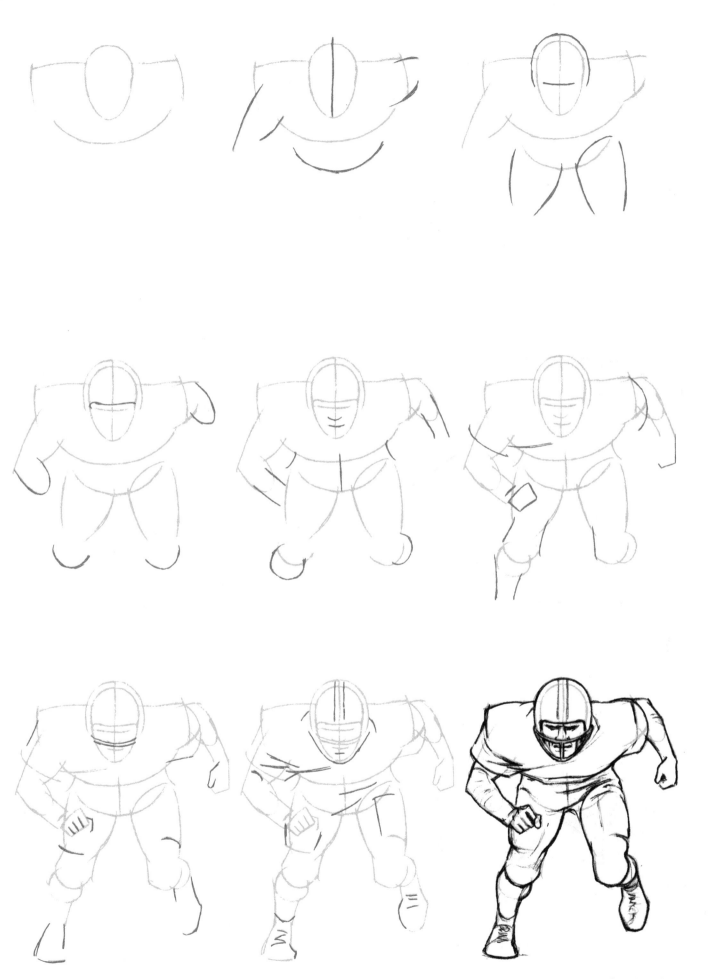

Football—linebacker

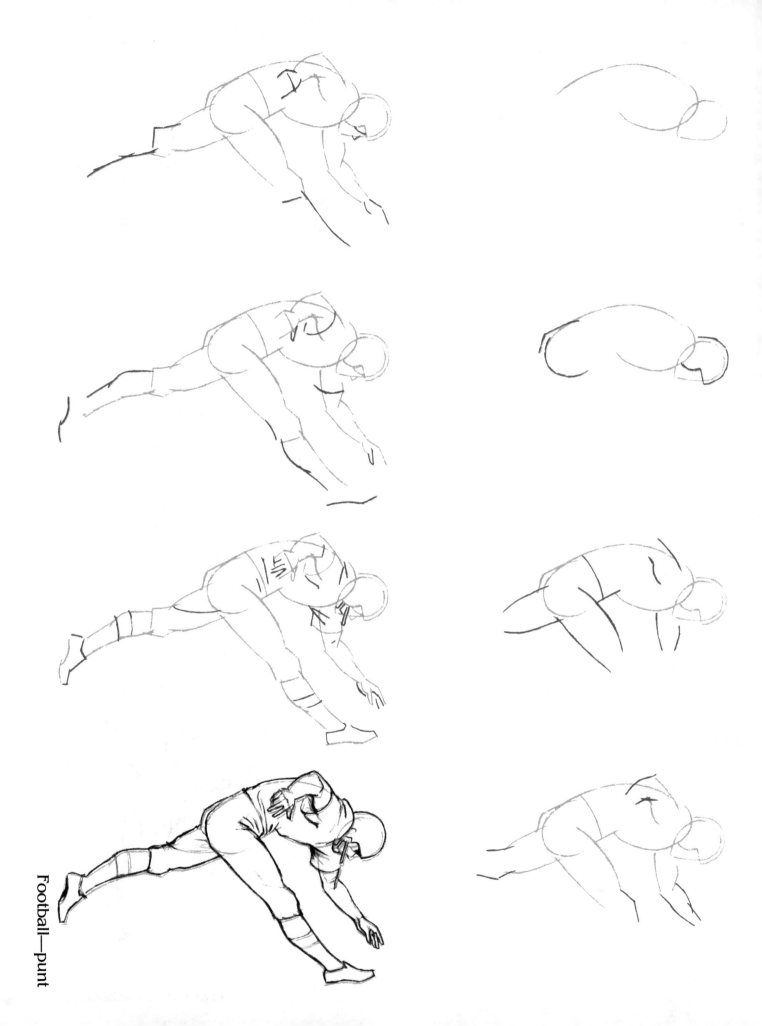

Football—punt

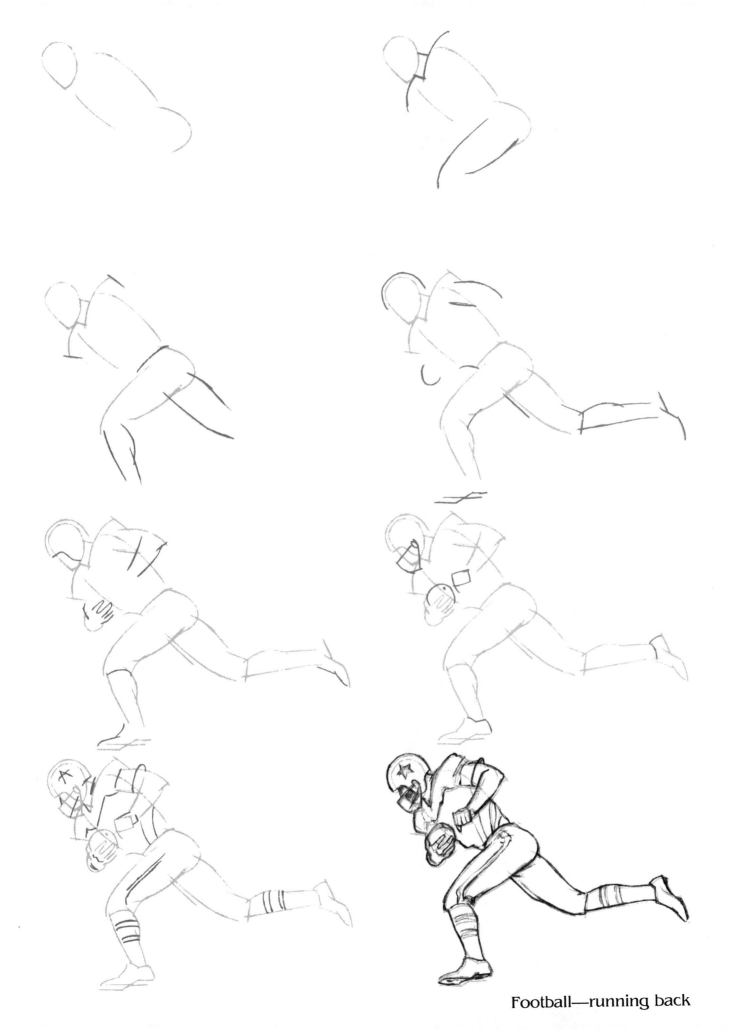

Football—running back

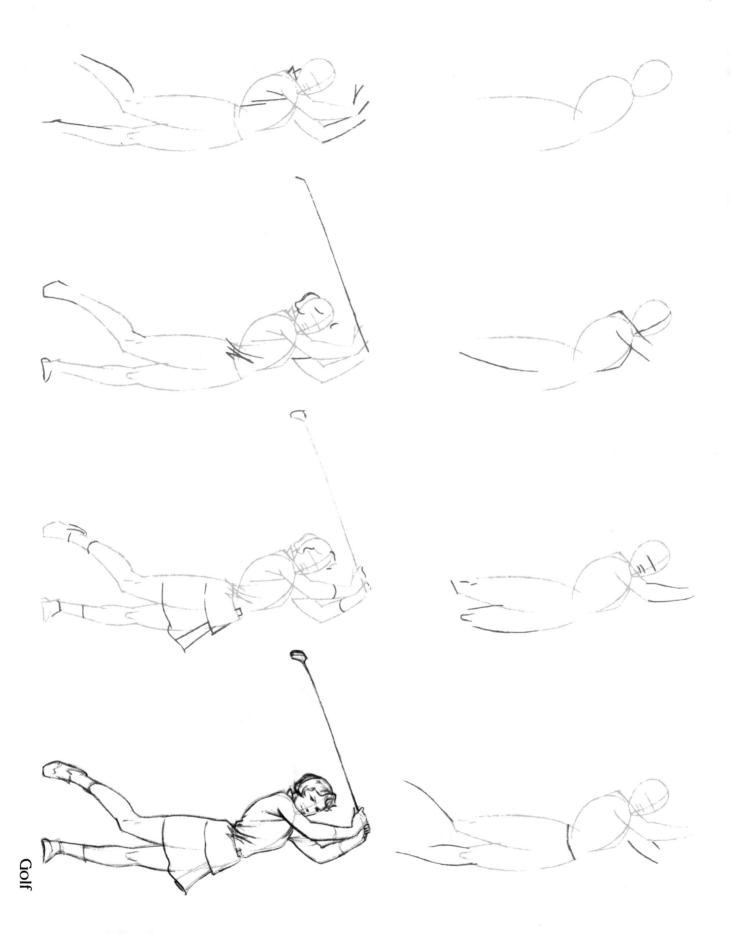

Golf

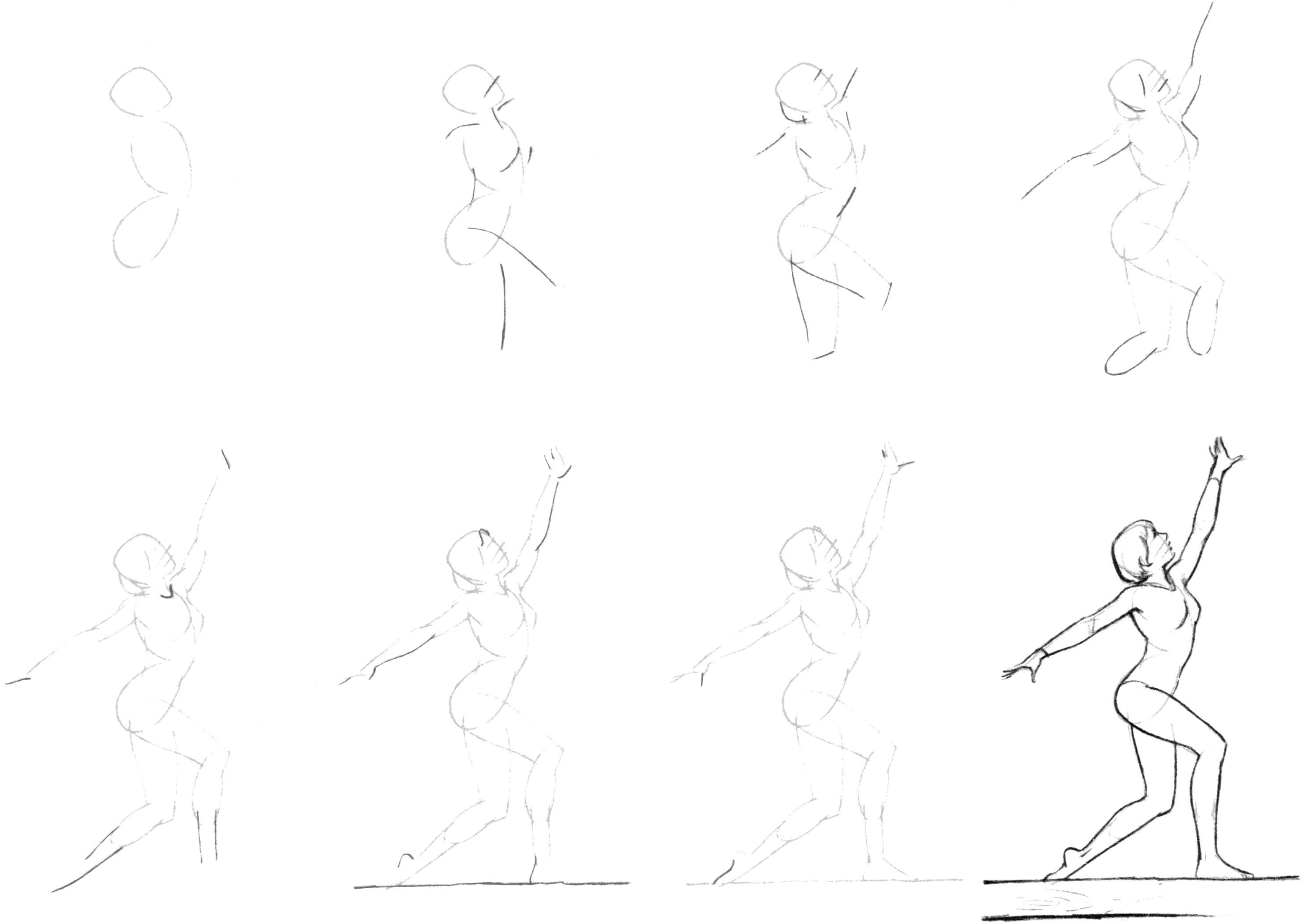

Gymnastics—balance beam

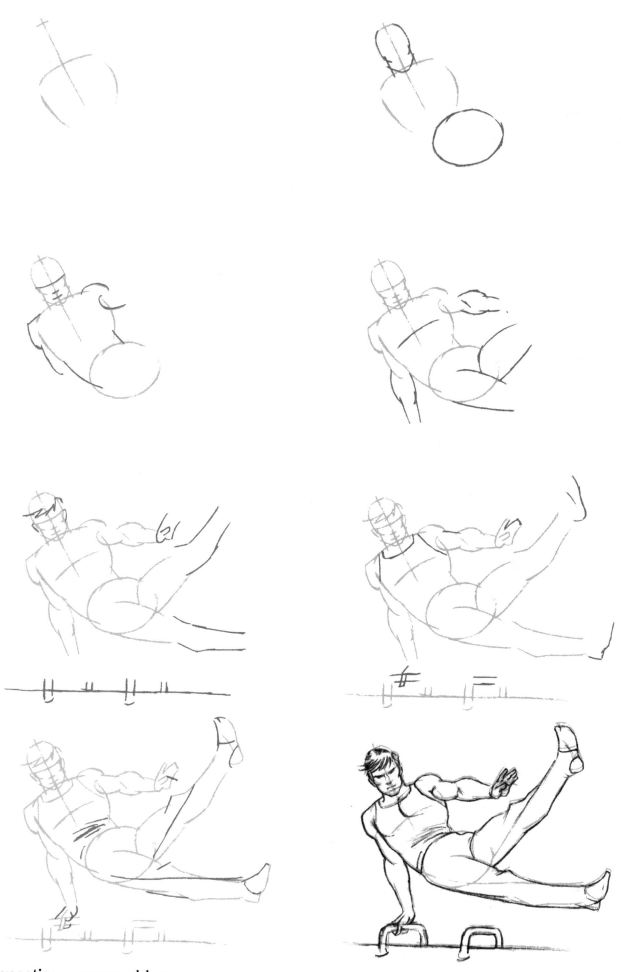

Gymnastics—pommel horse

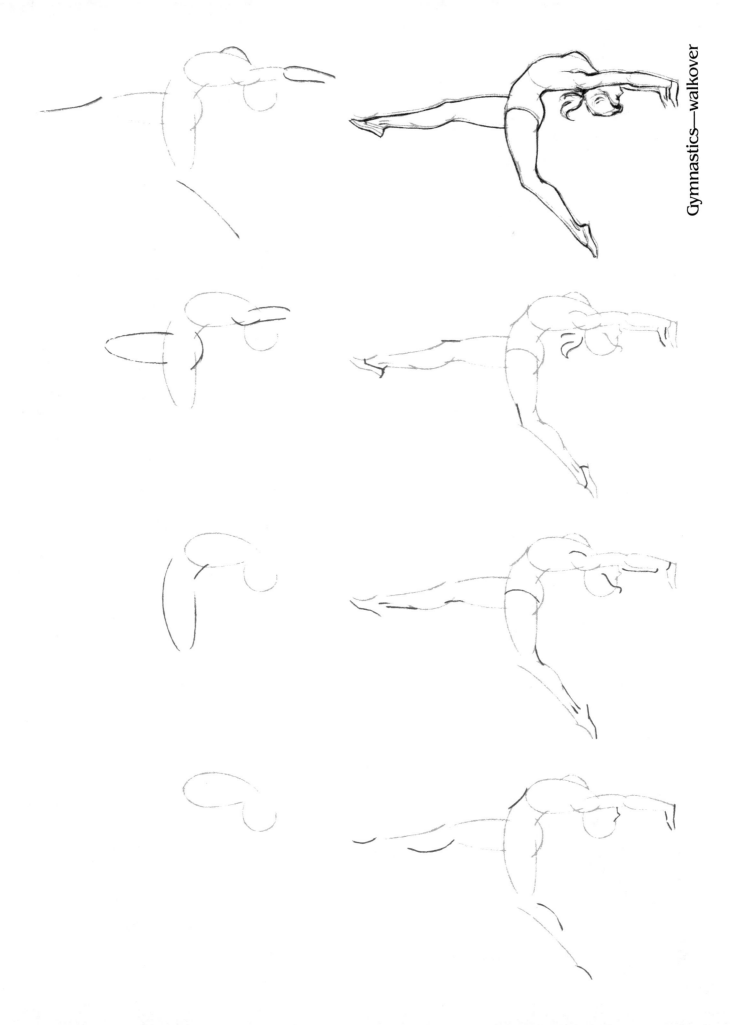

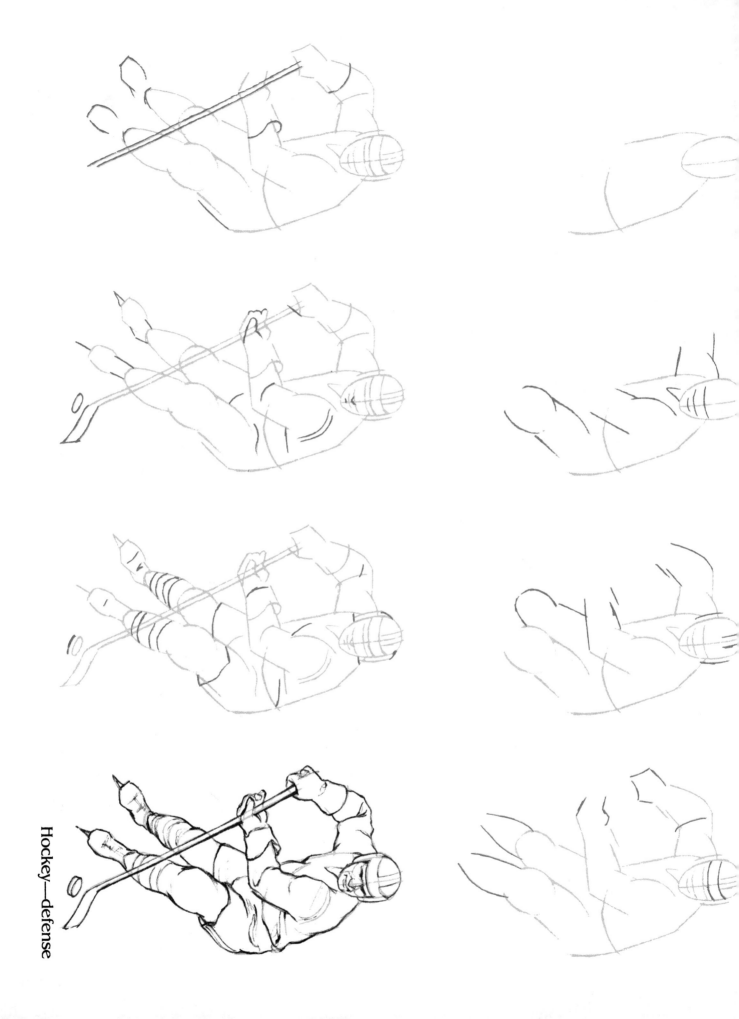

Hockey—defense

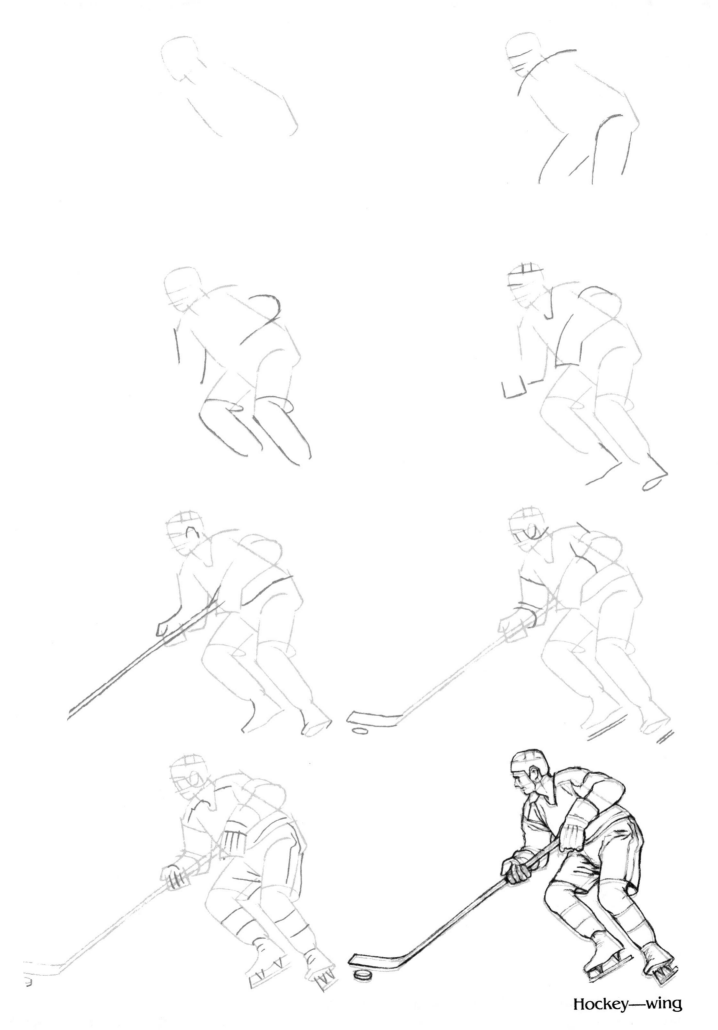

Hockey—wing

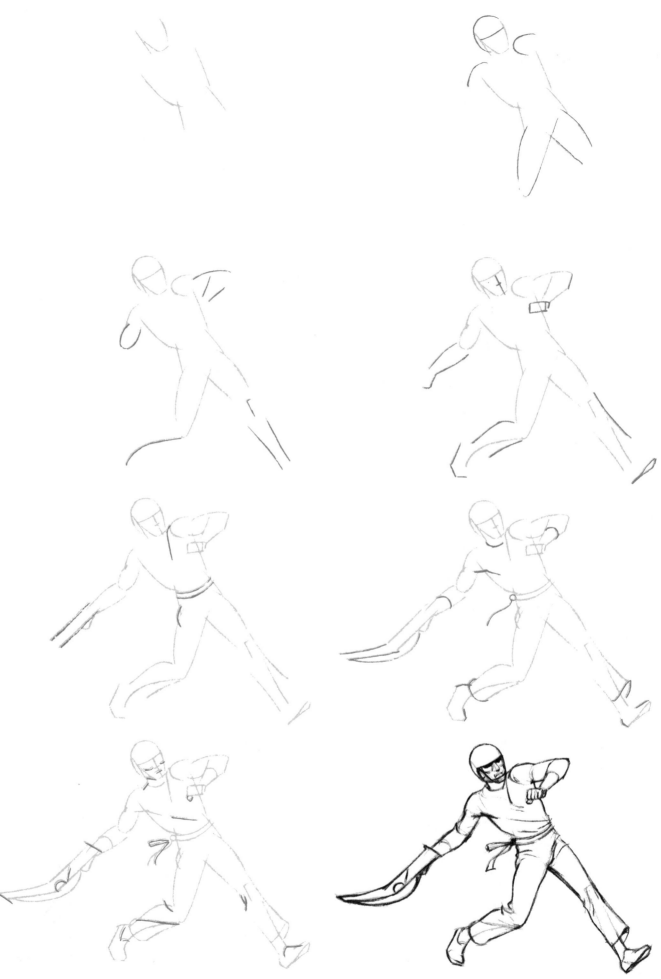

Jai Alai (Pelota)—atchiki (momentary holding of the pelote)

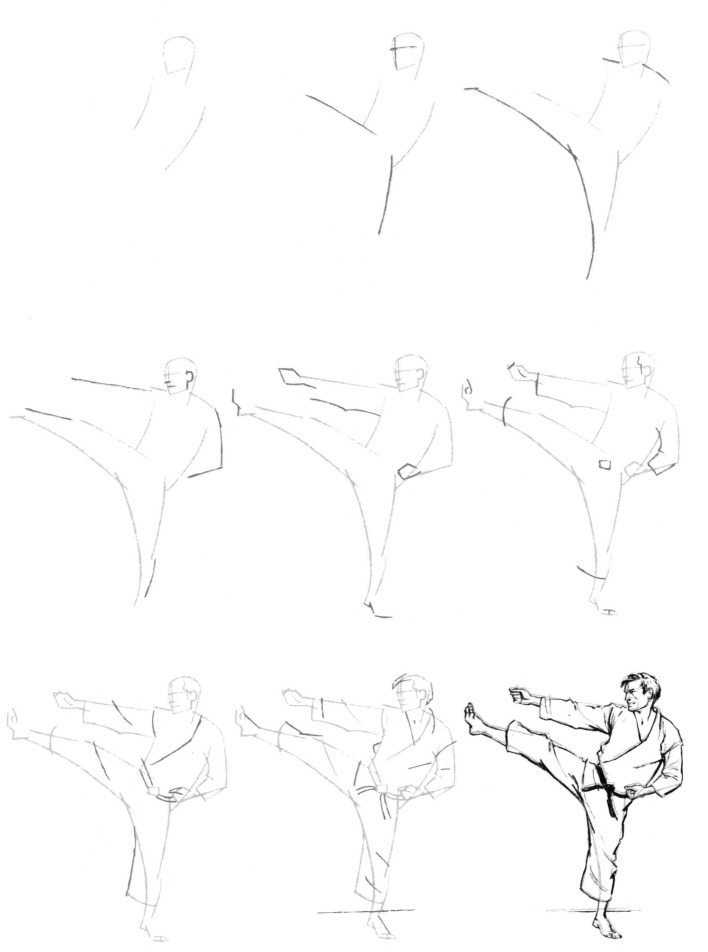

Karate—back fist & sword foot

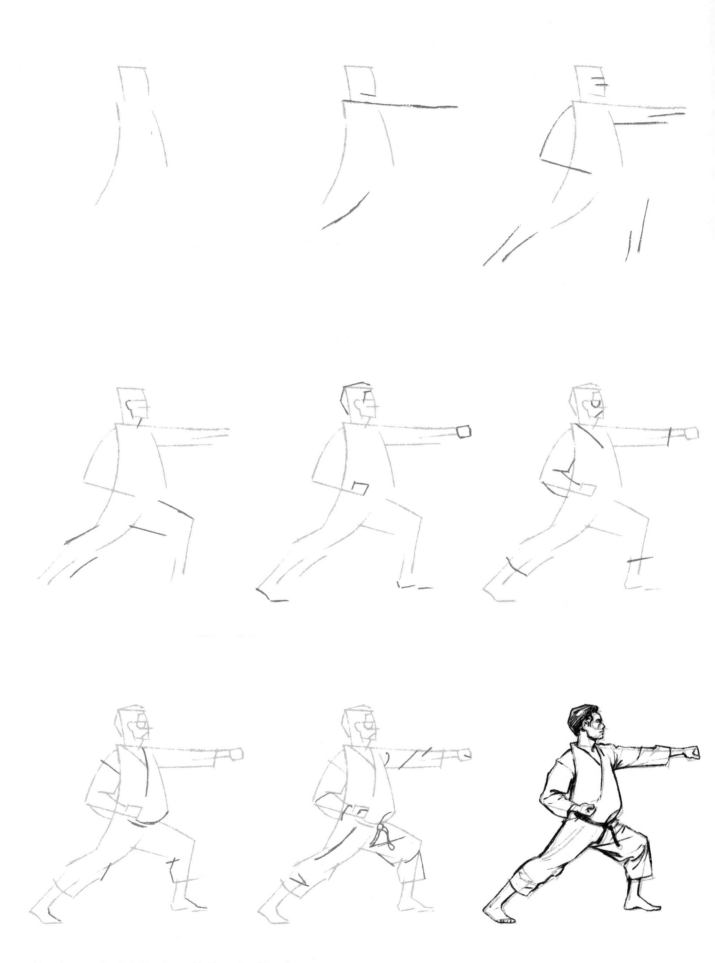

Karate—(middle level) front attack

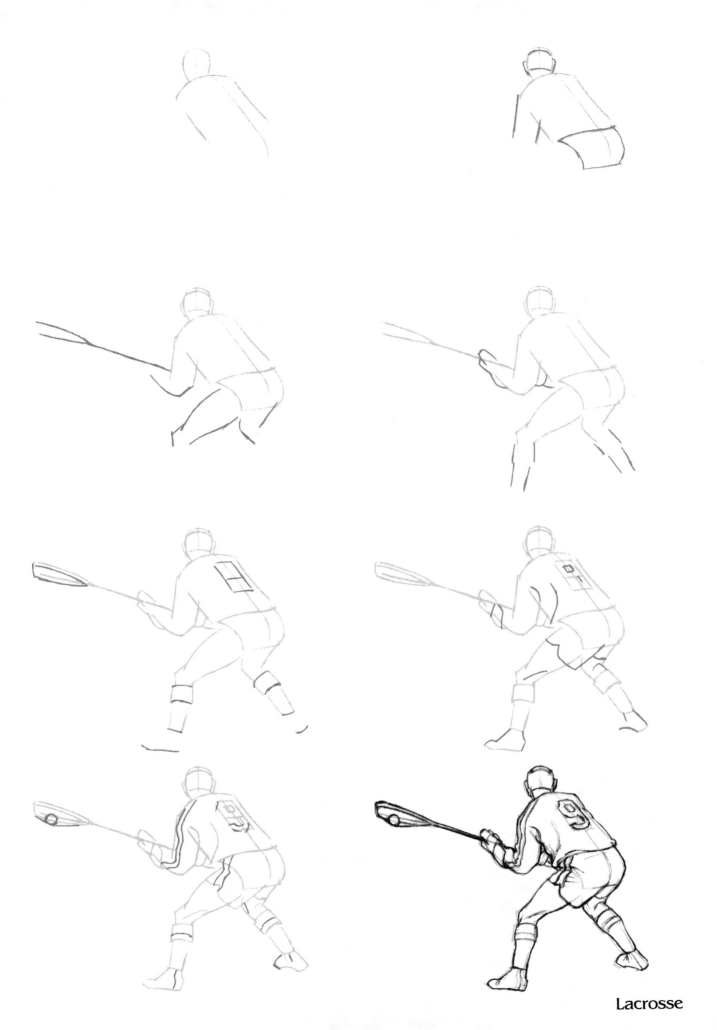

Lacrosse

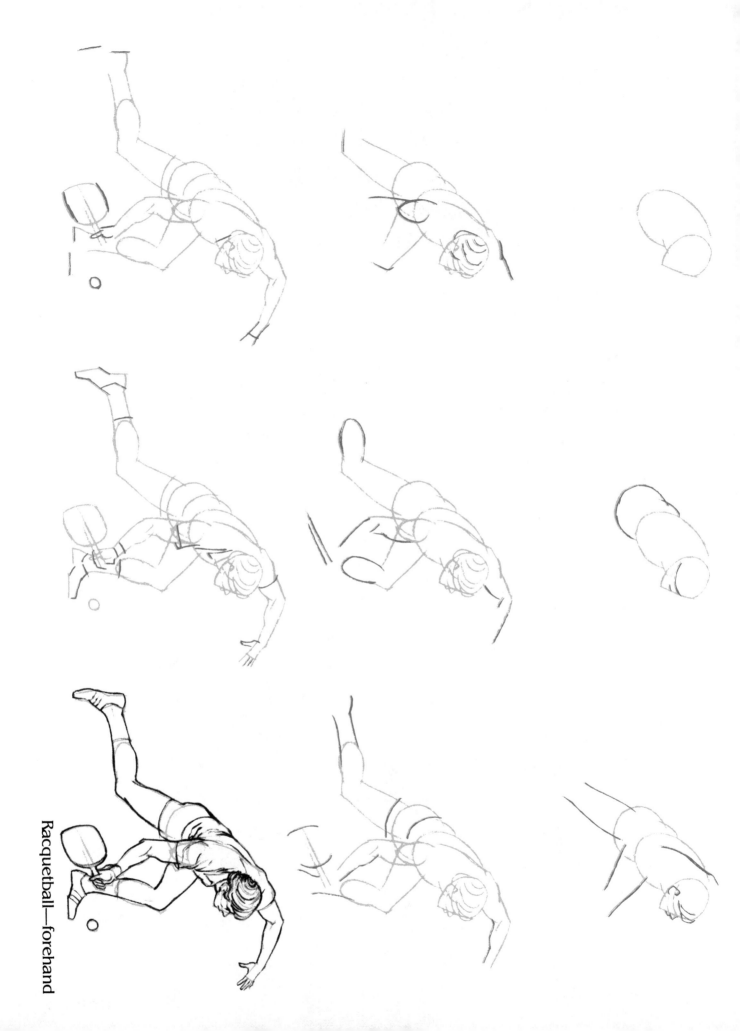

Racquetball—forehand

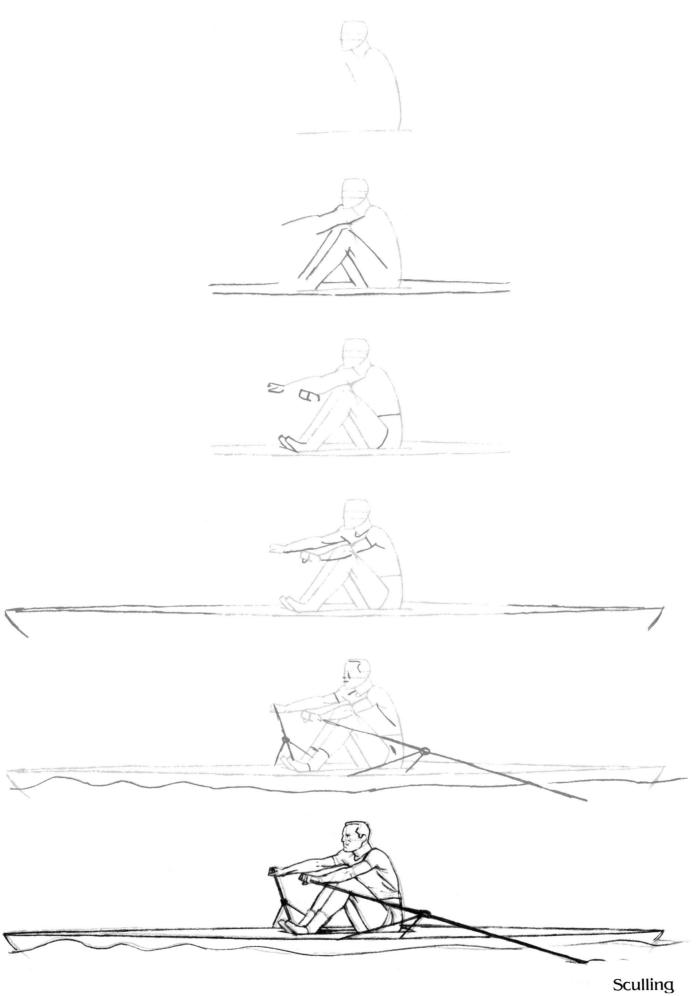

Sculling

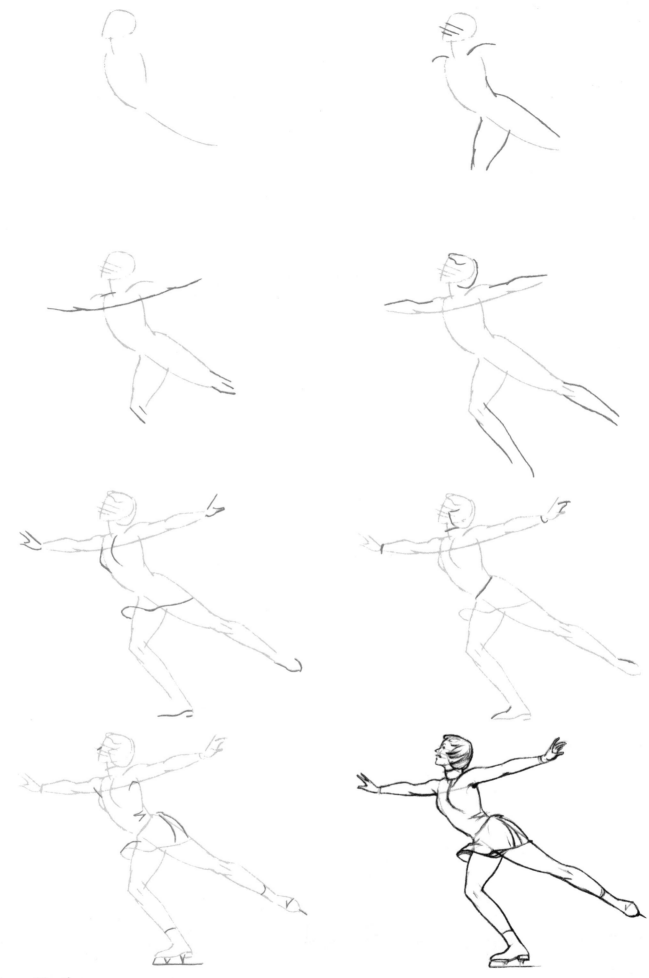

Figure Skating

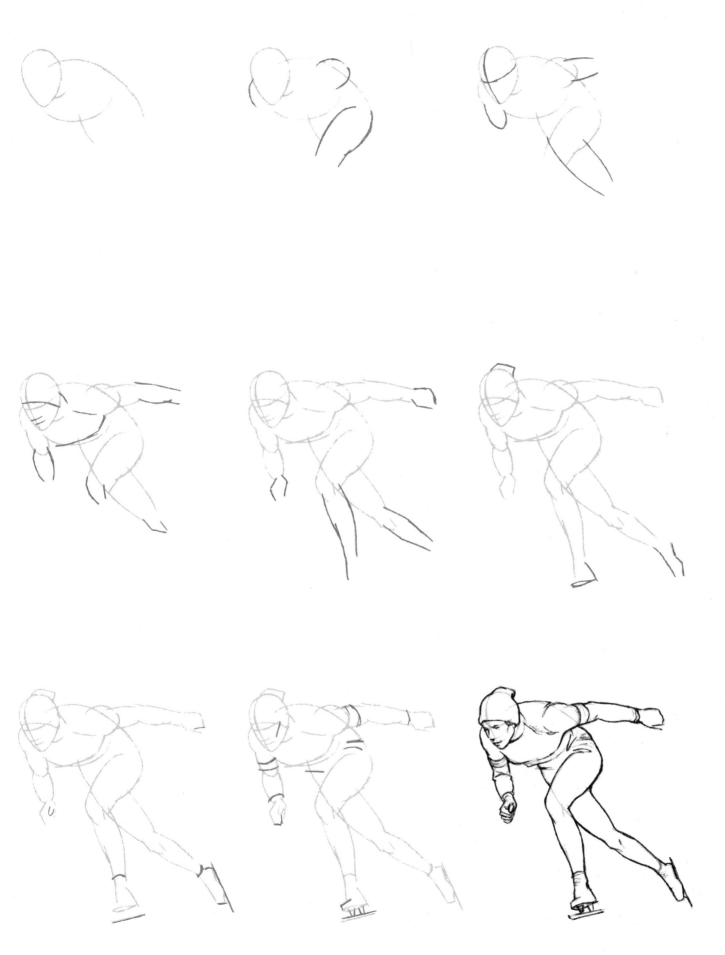

Skating—speed

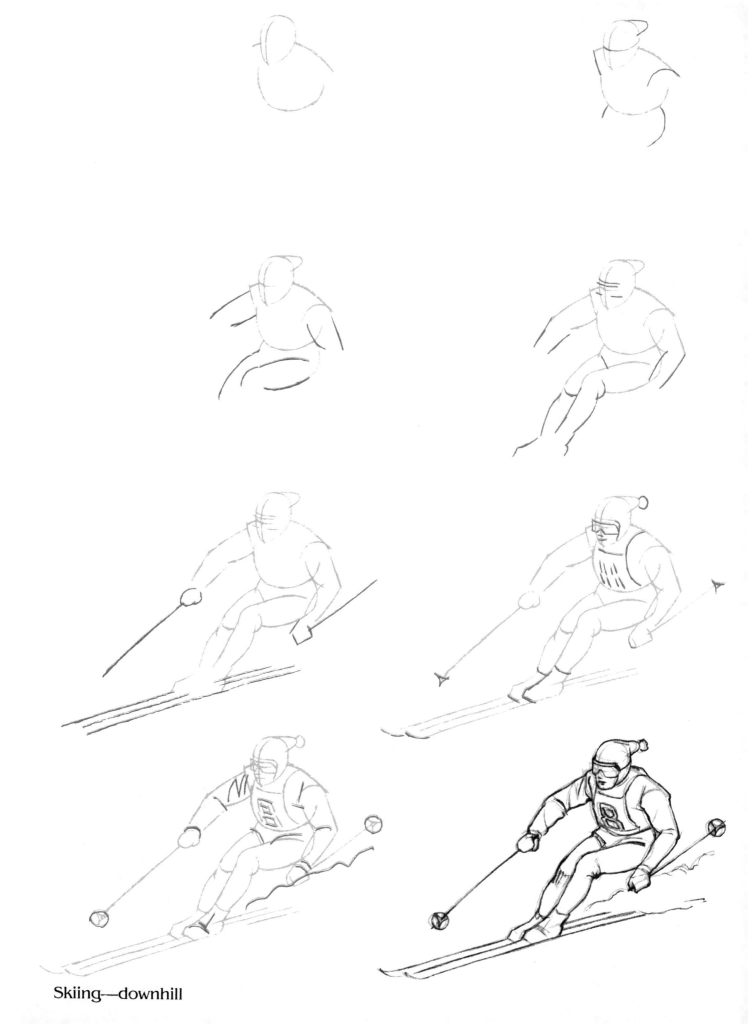

Skiing—downhill

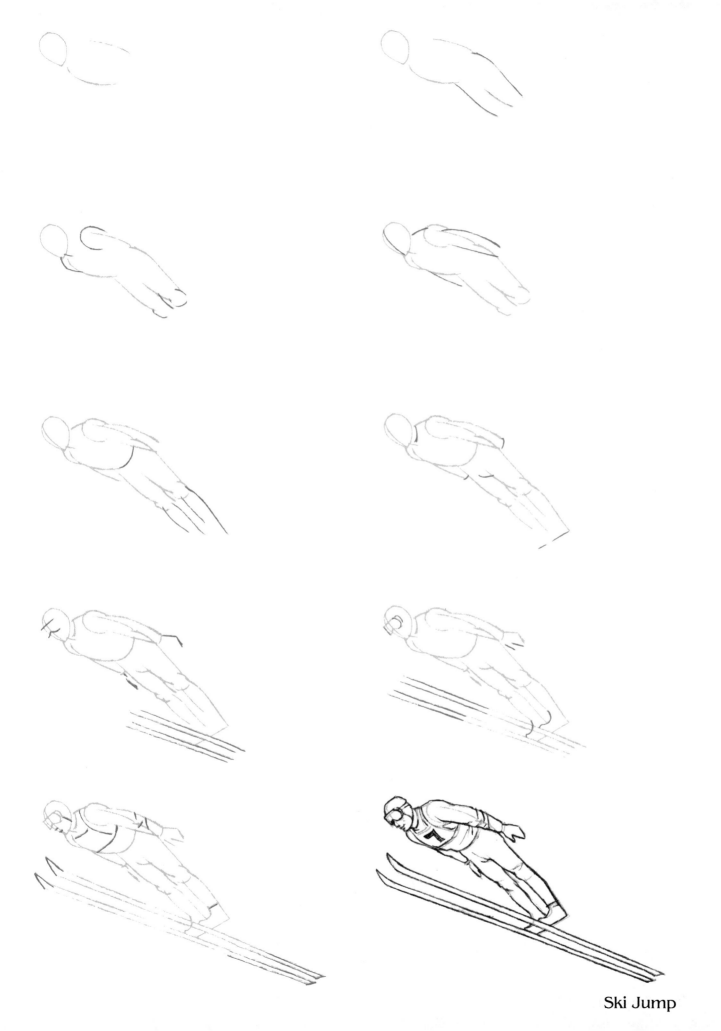

Ski Jump

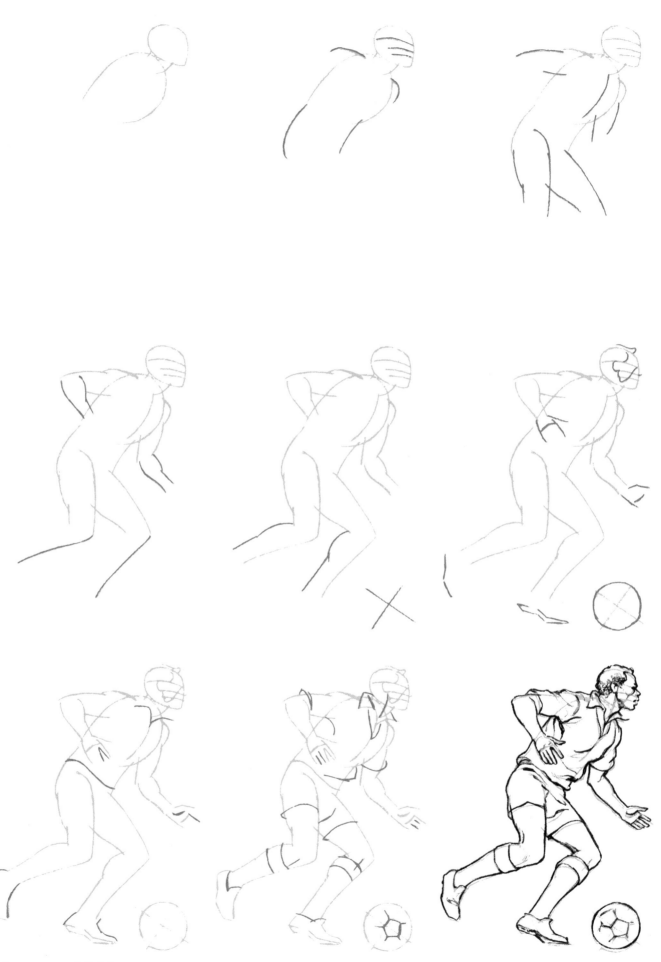

Soccer—dribble

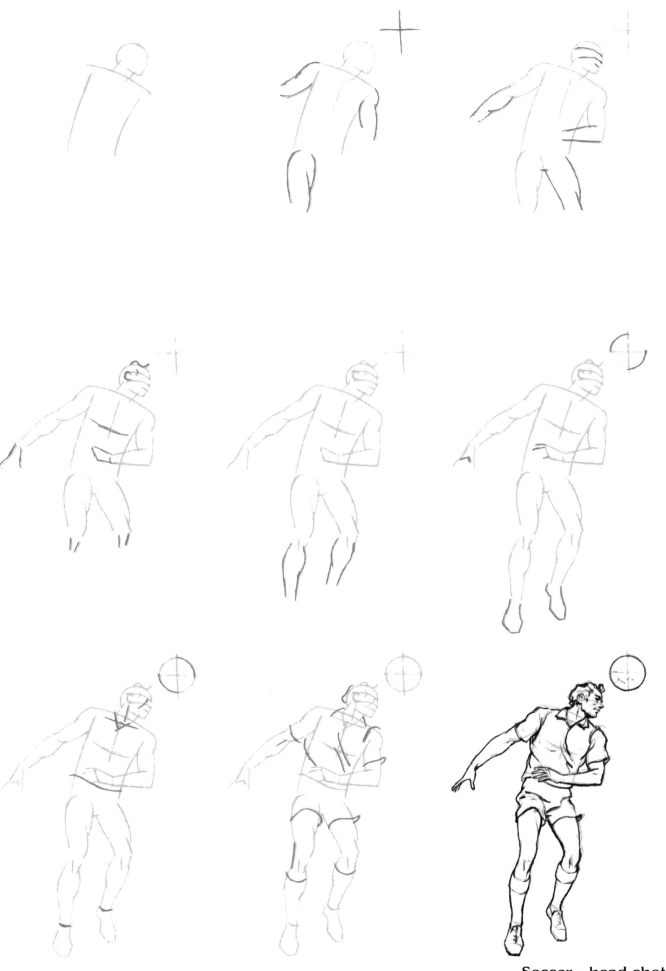

Soccer—head shot

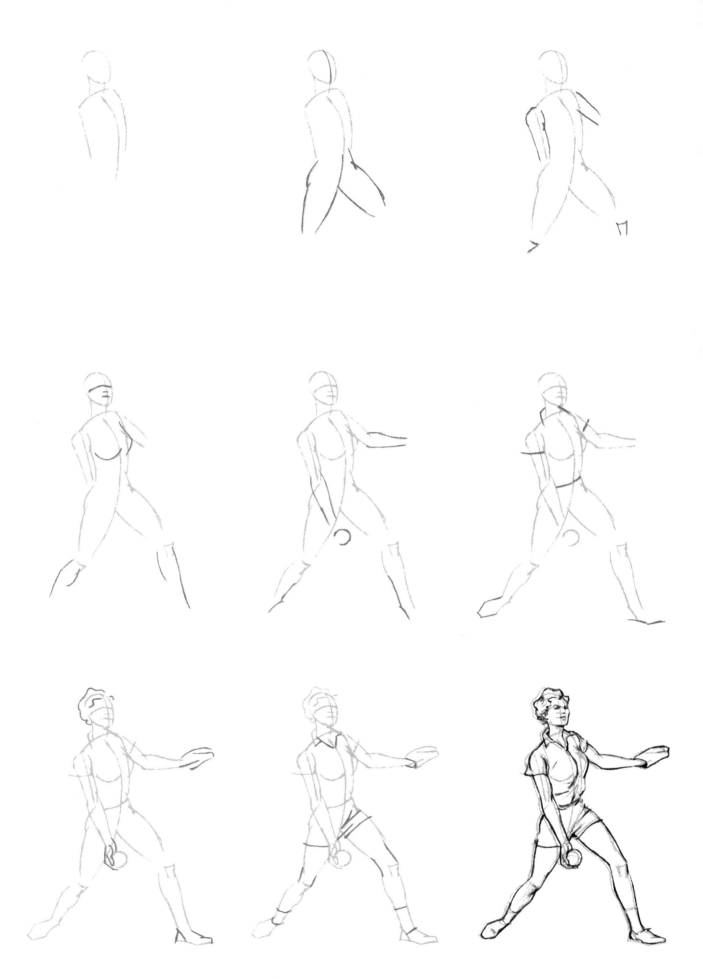

Softball—pitcher

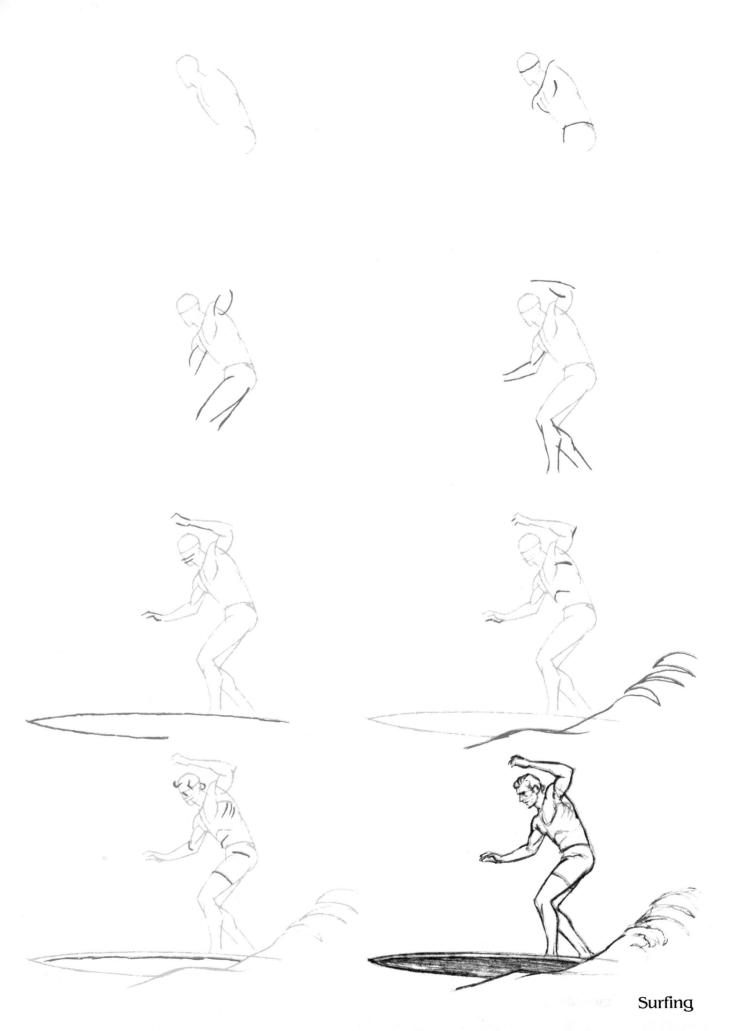

Surfing

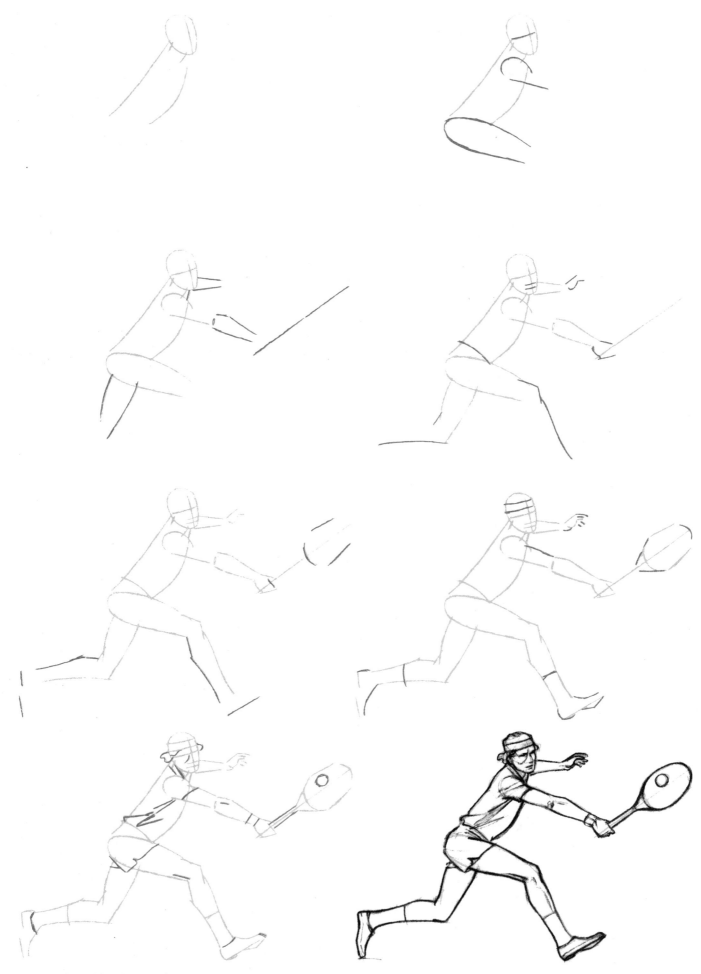

Tennis—backhand

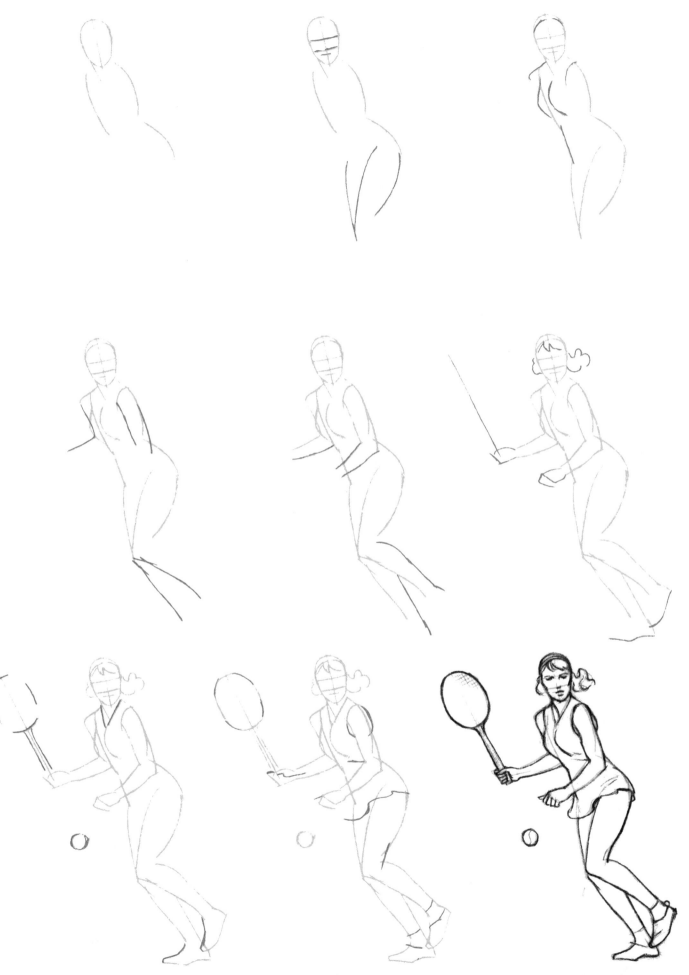

Tennis—forehand

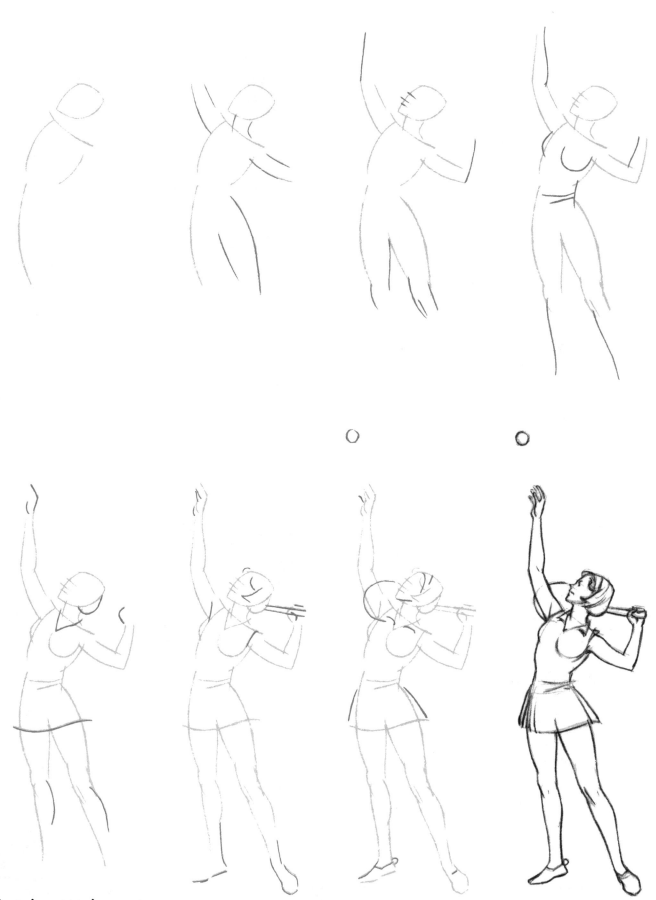

Tennis—service

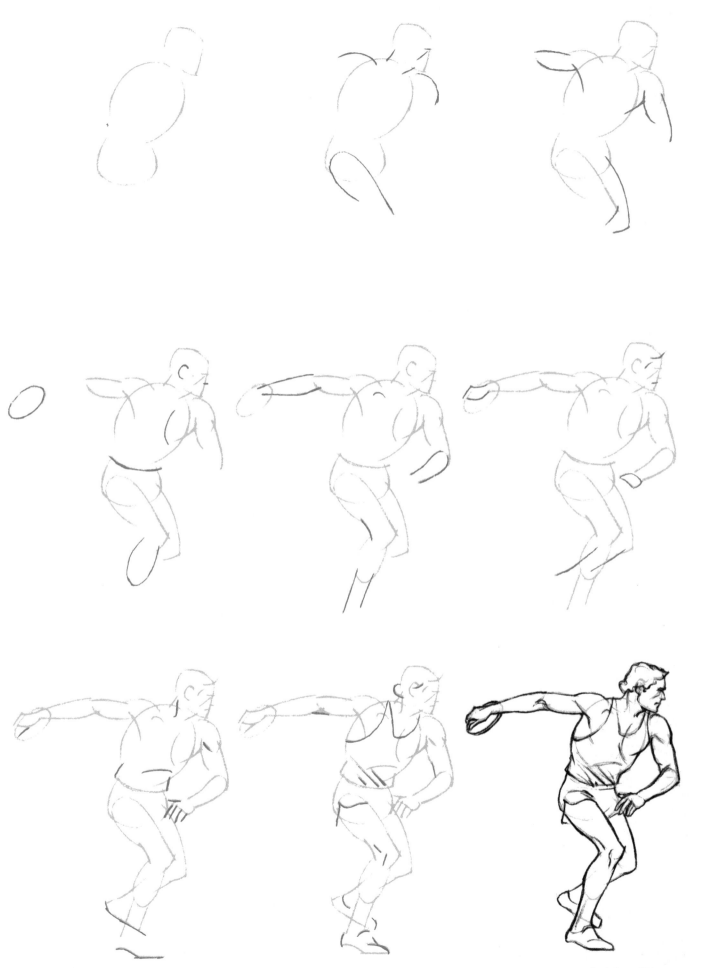

Track & Field—discus

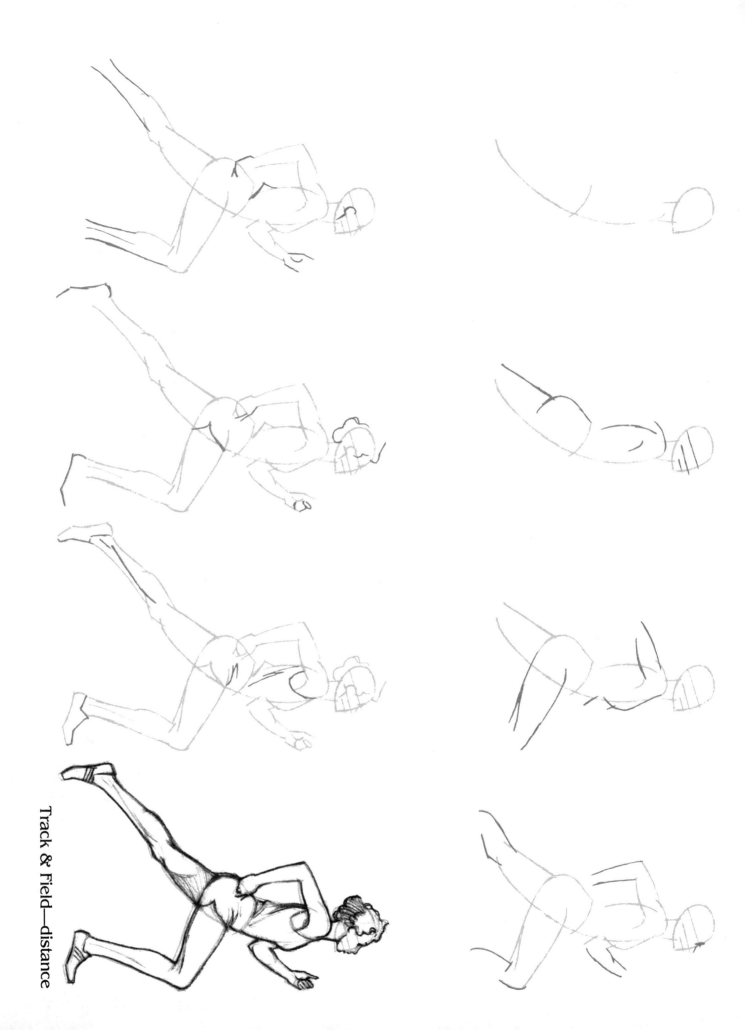

Track & Field—distance

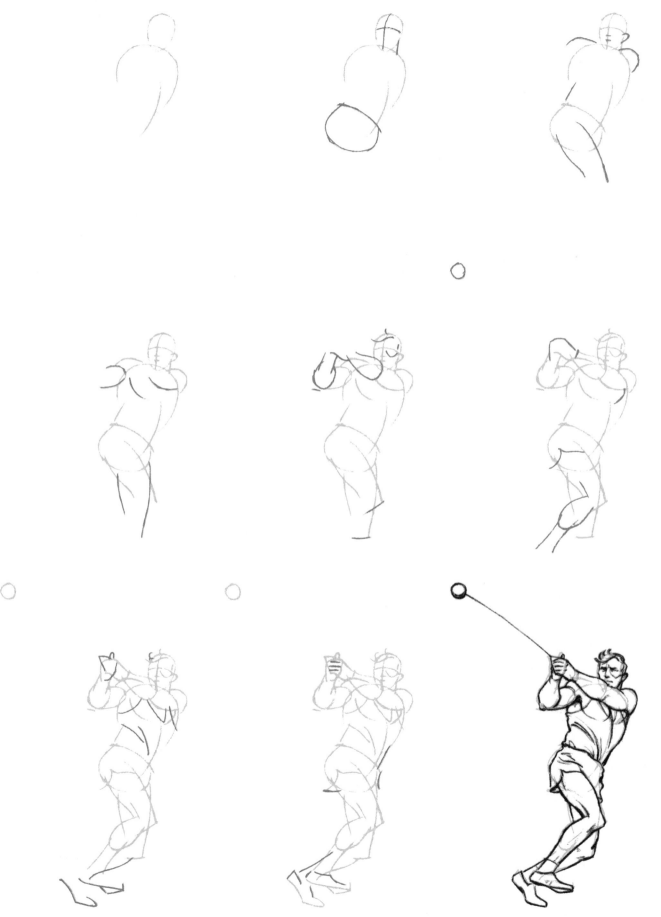

Track & Field—hammer throw

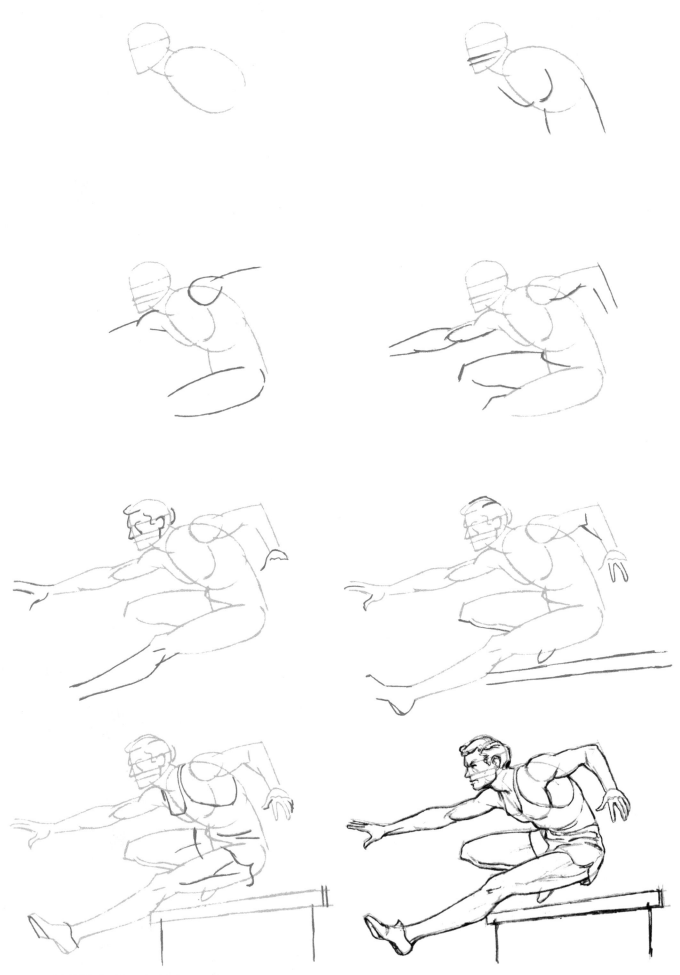

Track & Field—hurdles

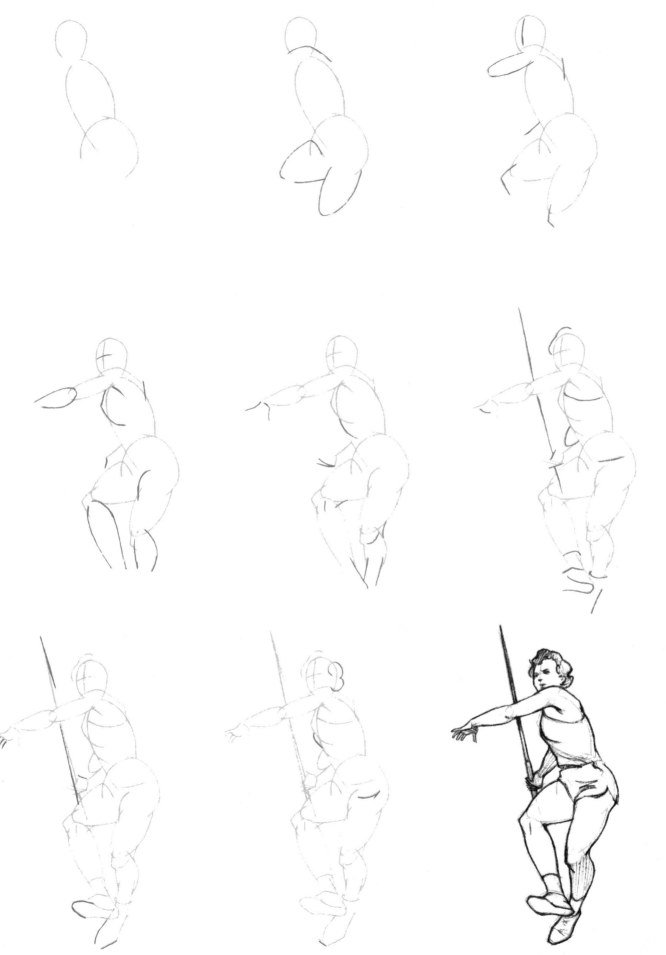

Track & Field—javelin

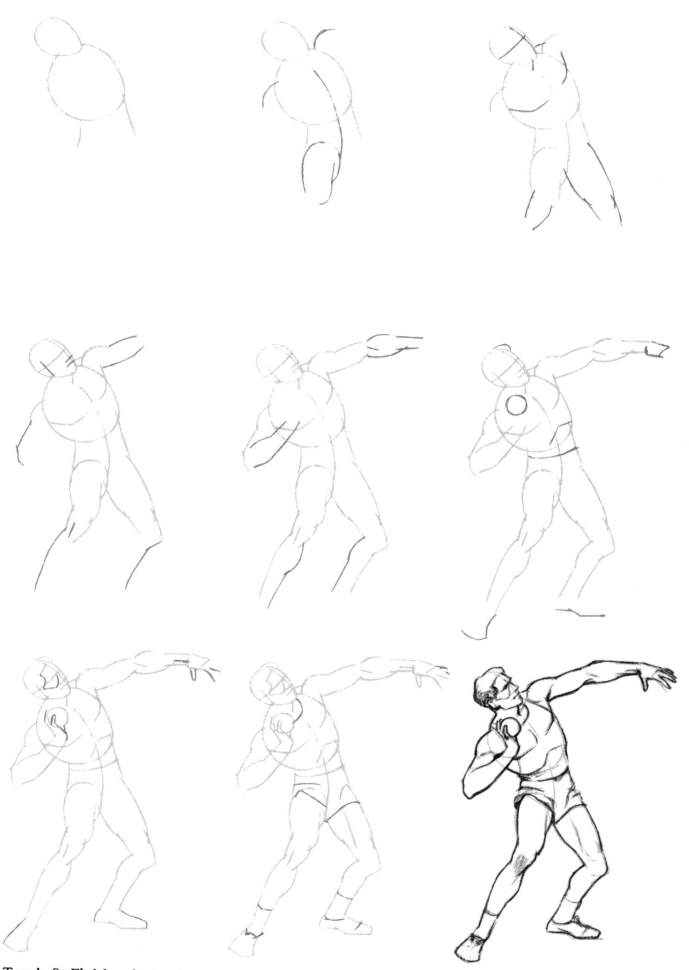

Track & Field—shotput

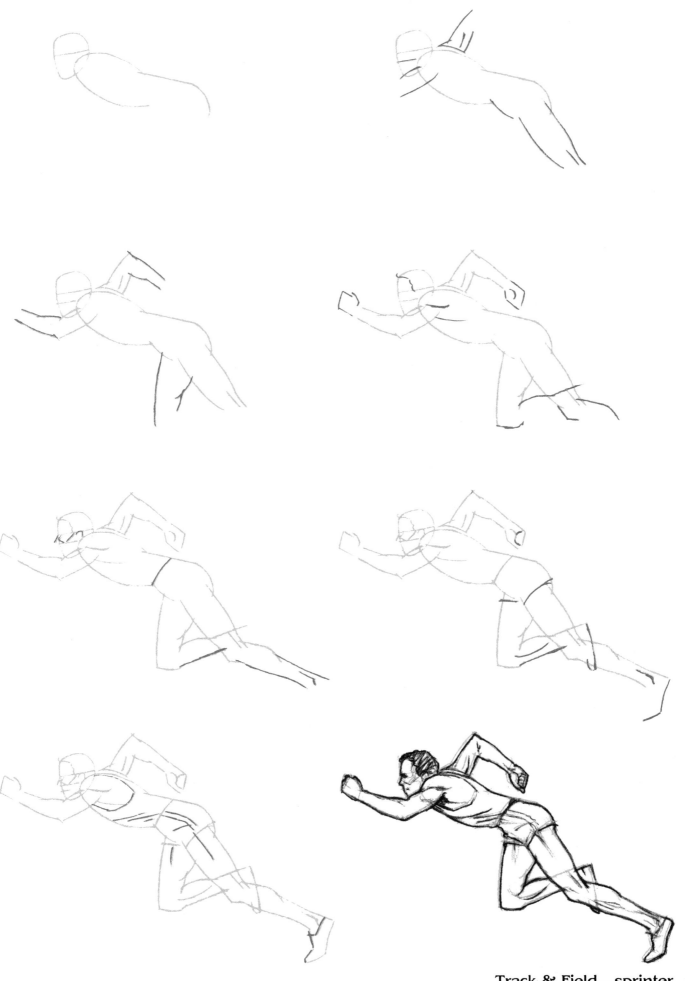

Track & Field—sprinter

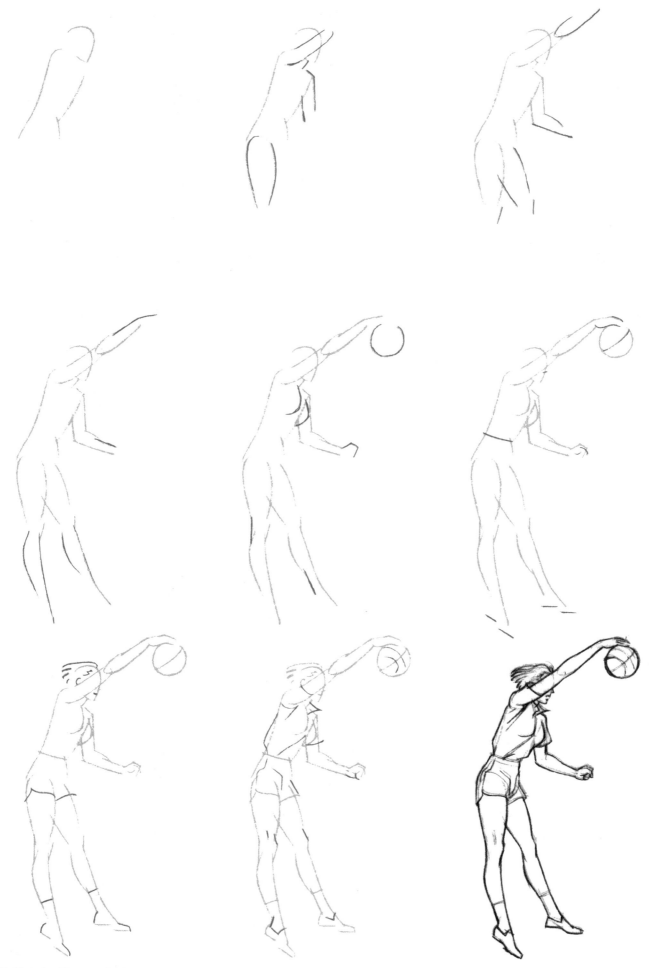

Volleyball—spike

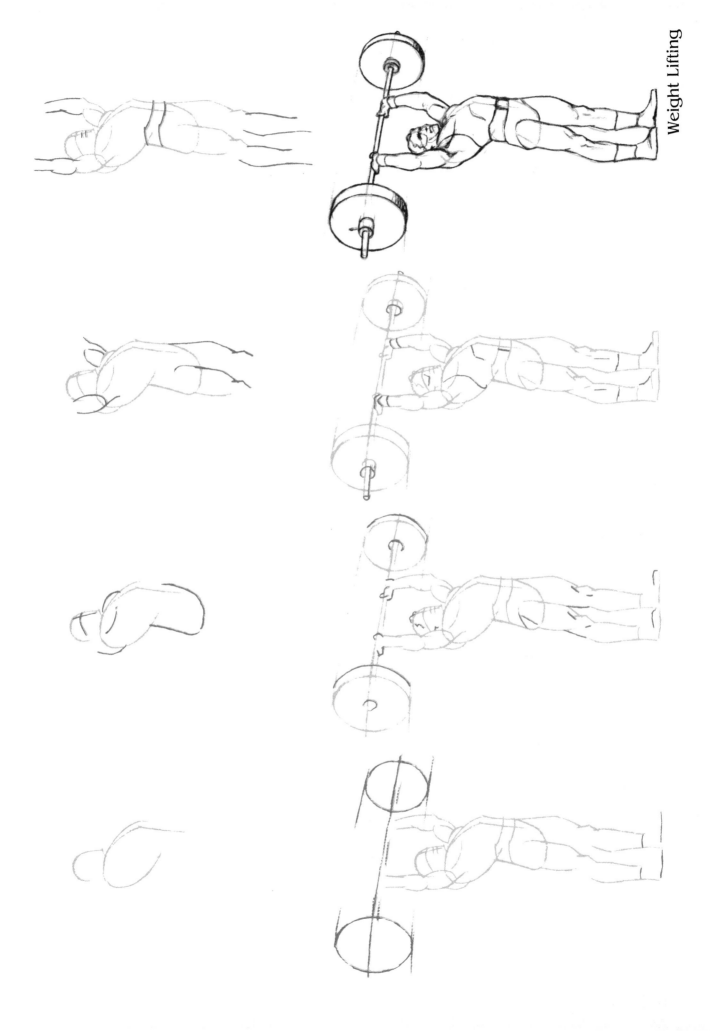

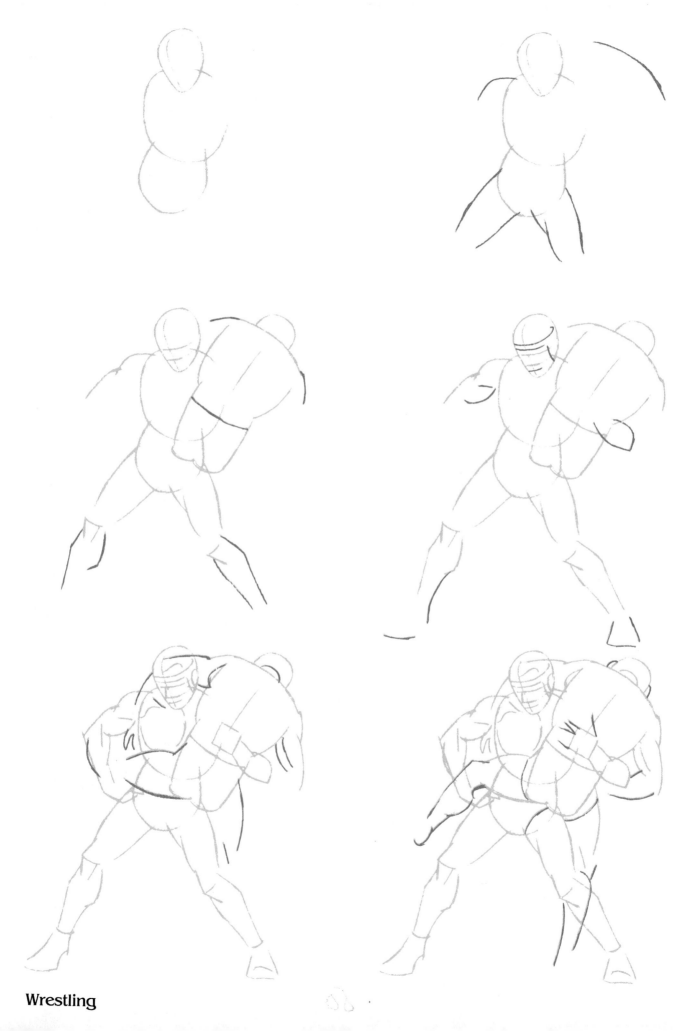

Wrestling

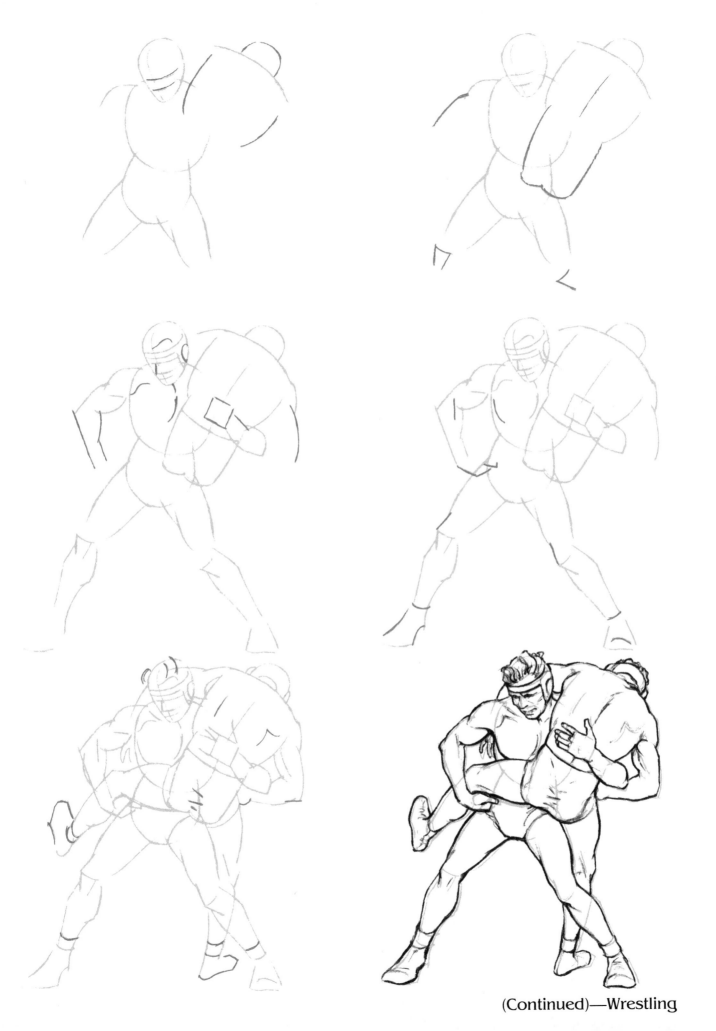

(Continued)—Wrestling

Lee J. Ames began his career at the Walt Disney Studios, working on films that included *Fantasia* and *Pinocchio*. He taught at the School of Visual Arts in Manhattan, and at Dowling College on Long Island, New York. An avid worker, Ames directed his own advertising agency, illustrated for several magazines, and illustrated approximately 150 books that range from picture books to postgraduate texts. He resided in Dix Hills, Long Island, with his wife, Jocelyn, until his death in June 2011.

DRAW 50 ATHLETES

Experience All That the Draw 50 Series Has to Offer!

With this proven, step-by-step method, Lee J. Ames has taught millions how to draw everything from amphibians to automobiles. Now it's your turn! Pick up the pencil, get out some paper, and learn how to draw everything under the sun with the Draw 50 series.

Also Available:

- *Draw 50 Airplanes, Aircraft, and Spacecraft*
- *Draw 50 Animals*
- *Draw 50 Baby Animals*
- *Draw 50 Cars, Trucks, and Motorcycles*
- *Draw 50 Flowers, Trees, and Other Plants*
- *Draw 50 Sharks, Whales, and Other Sea Creatures*
- *Draw 50 Vehicles*